Vintage Forrester:
Selected Writings From
The Daily Telegraph

Tony Forrester

B. T. Batsford Ltd, *London*

First published 1998

© Tony Forrester 1998

ISBN 0 7134 8292 3

A CIP catalogue record for this book is available from the British Library.

Typeset by Treadwell Publishing of Uttoxeter
Printed by Redwood Books, Trowbridge, Wiltshire
for the publishers,
B. T. Batsford Ltd, 583 Fulham Road,
London SW6 5BY

A BATSFORD BRIDGE BOOK
Series Editor: Tony Sowter
Commissioning Editor: Paul Lamford

CONTENTS

	Introduction	4
1	Second Hand Low, Maybe Not	5
2	How To Handle Your Trumps	15
3	Good Hand, Shame About The Result!	23
4	Conventions, Do We Need Them?	31
5	Tripping The High Wire	44
6	Weak or Strong 1NT?	50
7	Don't Be Nervous, It Won't Hurt	56
8	Defensive Posers, Are You On Form?	60
9	When to teach the opponents a lesson	72
10	What is a Mulligan?	80
11	Should You Use Hand Signals?	87
12	Sharpen Up Your Declarer Play	98
13	When To Flick The Switch	118
14	Well, Who Was The Greatest?	123
15	Can You Make The 'Opening Lead Team'	131

INTRODUCTION

It has been over four years since I began writing for the *Daily,* and more recently *Sunday, Telegraph.* In that time I have attempted to vary my style, providing a mixture of tournament reports, tips, quizzes plus a fair smattering of more light-hearted pieces. Inevitably, some of my efforts proved more popular than others.

This book is a distillation of my own personal favourites, plus those which captured your imagination, or at least appeared to, judging by your correspondence. Rather than simply serve up 'yesterday's· dinner', however, I have expanded on many of the points contained in the original articles, and, where possible, grouped together those which concentrate on a particular theme.

Finally, I have revisited the content, and tried to sharpen the 'English'. Not too tough that last bit!

I hope you will be thoroughly entertained and feel that you have picked up some valuable pointers. That is the idea!

1

SECOND HAND LOW, MAYBE NOT ...

Sometimes the best players in the world are caught napping, as this article from 1995 vividly shows.

Most of us have heard of 'third hand high' or 'second hand low'. They are rules which aid our defence, and which we can fall back on in times of crisis. But do they always hold good, and if not, how do we spot when to change our approach? It is a problem that we all share. Let's see what I am driving at:

North/South Game. Dealer South.

```
                    ♠ 73
                    ♡ Q6
                    ◇ Q10942
                    ♣ Q973
      ♠ K96          N          ♠ J10852
      ♡ KJ1042                  ♡ 987
      ◇ J3        W   E         ◇ 5
      ♣ A104         S          ♣ K652
                    ♠ AQ4
                    ♡ A53
                    ◇ AK876
                    ♣ J8
```

West	North	East	South
–	–	–	1◇
1♡	2◇	2♡	2NT
3♡	5◇	All Pass	

West led ♡J and was disappointed to see dummy's queen hold the trick. Declarer drew trumps and then led a low club from dummy, putting up ♣J

when East played low. West returned a heart, declarer won ♡A and ran
♣8 losing to the king.

East played a spade through, but declarer guessed correctly to rise with
♠A, cross to dummy and cash ♣Q, hoping the ten would fall. When it
did, *both* losing spades could be discarded from hand, and the contract
came home. Did East/West go wrong or was the declarer too good for
them? Think about that while you look at our second hand.

Love All. Dealer South.

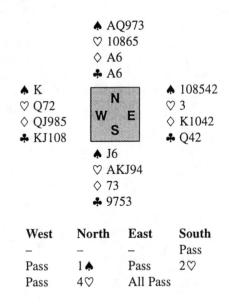

```
              ♠ AQ973
              ♡ 10865
              ◇ A6
              ♣ A6
  ♠ K                        ♠ 108542
  ♡ Q72          N          ♡ 3
  ◇ QJ985      W   E        ◇ K1042
  ♣ KJ108         S          ♣ Q42
              ♠ J6
              ♡ AKJ94
              ◇ 73
              ♣ 9753
```

West	North	East	South
–	–	–	Pass
Pass	1♠	Pass	2♡
Pass	4♡	All Pass	

West led ◇Q, declarer won in dummy, crossed to ♡A and led out ♠J to
the king and ace. Next came ♣A and a club which went to West's ♣10.
He continued with a diamond to his partner's king who then switched back
to clubs. Declarer ruffed in dummy, played a trump to the king and ruffed
his last club.

The defence could take its master trump whenever it wished. Again, the
play seems reasonably routine, and yet on both hands East missed a
chance to defeat the contract by doing the unnatural thing. *Second hand
high!*

On the first example, if East had risen with ♣K immediately and switched to a spade, declarer would have faced inevitable defeat. The club winners in dummy cannot be set up before the defence takes ♠K.

On our second hand, if East rises with ♣Q on the second round, he can lead a spade for his partner to ruff, regain the lead with ◇K and play another spade promoting ♡Q as the defence's fourth trick.

If you missed these plays, do not worry because you are in the company of two of the world's finest card players, Paul Hackett (from the Crockford's Final) and Zia Mahmood (from the Cavendish Pairs). The key was that East required an early entry.

However, the degree of difficulty was vastly heightened by the fact that the lead came from dummy, and hence neither 'East' actually knew that he could win the trick even if he played his honour. But then, declarer isn't there to make the defence's life easy!

Notice that point about declarer leading from dummy and thus keeping the defenders in the dark. Recently, Andrew Robson, the British International, faced a similarly tricky problem, and came up with the wrong answer. Try your luck:

North/South Game. Dealer South.

```
                    ♠ A432
                    ♡ K762
                    ◇ 832
                    ♣ K4
              ┌───────────┐      ♠ QJ7
              │     N     │      ♡ AJ9843
              │  W     E  │      ◇ A75
              │     S     │      ♣ 6
              └───────────┘
```

West	North	East	South
–	–	–	1♣
1◇	1♡	3◇	4♣
Pass	5♣	Dble	All Pass

Robson (East) does not like to be trifled with, so he took exception to being brushed aside in the auction and doubled 5♣.

When partner cashed ◇ KQ for the first two tricks, everything looked rosy in the garden. What could possibly go wrong? West switched to ♠ 10 at trick three and declarer won ♠ A before leading a low heart.

Time stood still, while Robson debated whether to rise with the ace and play South for:

> ♠ K5
> ♡ Q
> ◇ J6
> ♣ AQJ108752

or follow with a low heart, and hope that declarer held:

> ♠ K65
> ♡ –
> ◇ J6
> ♣ AQJ108752

Well, what is it to be? Before you answer, I will give you a small clue, consider your partner's action at trick three.

The full layout was:

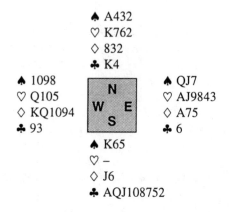

```
                    ♠ A432
                    ♡ K762
                    ◇ 832
                    ♣ K4
    ♠ 1098                          ♠ QJ7
    ♡ Q105        N                ♡ AJ9843
    ◇ KQ1094   W     E             ◇ A75
    ♣ 93          S                ♣ 6
                    ♠ K65
                    ♡ –
                    ◇ J6
                    ♣ AQJ108752
```

East selected ♡A, at which point South leant forward with the words 'Wrong, I'm afraid'. Did East guess unluckily, or was there a clue to the winning play?

The answer lies in West's decision to switch to a spade. If his heart holding was ♡105 as East actually played for, he would probably have led the suit at trick three, confident that his partner held ♡A for his double of 5♣. West's spade switch meant that he had hearts sewn up.

Note that if West does lead hearts, he must play ♡Q. If he chooses ♡5, East will not know whether it is a singleton or from ♡Q105 and may well go wrong.

However, credit South with a good play and note he put the pressure on before the defence had a chance to signal their distribution.

The tactic of leading towards your (declarer's) hand is a good one, and cannot be over-estimated. In 1991, I was invited to produce a tip for BOLS, the Dutch drinks company. The idea was that the advice given would have general application and I concentrated on 'Leading towards the closed (declarer's) hand'. Here it is, see what you think:

The Power of the Closed Hand

We have all faced the situation on many occasions. Dummy has xxx in a suit and leads to declarer's king. We (over declarer) have Axx. To win or not to win?

If we take the ace, declarer has KQ10 and now finesses against partner's jack, when he would almost certainly go wrong if his king had held. If we duck, declarer has Kxx and needs that trick for the contract!

The problem is not exactly original I agree, but this type of situation is a common variation on a theme which extends to many hands. It is the tip of the iceberg:

Consider these hands:

♠ J107
♡ AJ5
◇ AQ62
♣ K64

```
    N
  W   E
    S
```

♠ KQ6
♡ KQ10
◇ 8753
♣ A52

You are playing, not surprisingly, in 3NT and West leads ♠2 (fourth highest). Clearly the contract depends upon the diamond suit which in technical terms should be tackled by cashing the ace, coming to hand and leading up to the queen. However, a more practical line is to win ♠J at trick one and lead a low diamond from dummy. East is obviously under pressure with Kx, as he is unaware that the entire hand depends upon the suit. Even with Kxx he may be tempted to put up the king to play a spade through to partner's imagined ♠Kxx or ♠AQx.

A defender has been forced to guess the holding of a suit in the closed hand without any real clue. That is the basis of my tip:

Whenever you can, use the power of the closed hand.

If you are confident of the location of the high cards, even more can be done. Try leading from K10xxx in dummy towards a low singleton in hand, should you be certain that the ace is on your right. How can he tell you do not have a singleton queen? Even if your opponent has ace-queen you may persuade him to put up the queen, giving you a chance to ruff out Jxx in his partner's hand.

With KQxxx opposite a void, don't automatically lead the king for a ruffing finesse, it may be better to lead a low one first, testing your right hand opponent. After all, you may have a singleton jack. If he plays low smoothly, that is a good clue as to the location of the ace.

Love All. Dealer North.

```
              ♠ Q
              ♡ AK42
              ◇ Q74
              ♣ A7542

                   N
              W         E
                   S

              ♠ A85432
              ♡ J7
              ◇ KJ5
              ♣ QJ
```

West	North	East	South
–	1♣	Pass	1♠
Pass	2♣	Pass	3♠
Pass	4♠	All Pass	

I played this hand in 4♠ after a typical sequence to the wrong contract. A diamond to the ace and another diamond left me with the problem of how to broach spades. Do you have any ideas?

Trying to create some confusion in the enemy ranks, I won ◇K and crossed to dummy with a heart to lead ♠Q. East (with ♠K97) could not understand why I had gone to the apparent effort of crossing to dummy to lead spades unless I had something like AJ10xxx (he knew I had at least six from the bidding). So he ducked and I stole a trick. How could he tell what to do? The answer is that he couldn't! He was forced to guess because declarer gave the impression of holding a different hand.

Lead from dummy as often as possible even when there may appear to be little advantage. It is strange how often you set the defenders a problem which you may not have seen yourself.

My final hand illustrates exactly what I mean:

♠ K52
♡ A107
◇ A75
♣ 10943

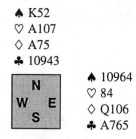

♠ 10964
♡ 84
◇ Q106
♣ A765

You are East, defending 6NT on a sequence of 2NT (20-22) – 4NT – 6NT. Partner leads the seven of spades to dummy's king, declarer following with the jack. A club from dummy goes to declarer's king and partner's two. Now ♡J is overtaken by dummy's ace, to be followed by ♣10 and you?

Declarer appears to have AQJ, KQJ, KJxx, KQx to make sense of the bidding and play, so you (as actually happened at the table), play low. However, the full hand was:

♠ K52
♡ A107
◇ A75
♣ 10943

♠ 873
♡ 652
◇ J932
♣ J82

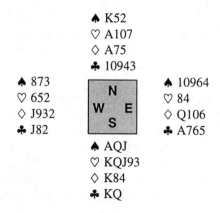

♠ 10964
♡ 84
◇ Q106
♣ A765

♠ AQJ
♡ KQJ93
◇ K84
♣ KQ

Declarer was originally trying to rectify the count for a minor suit squeeze and failing that, hoped ♣J was doubleton. He did not really see why he arranged to lead clubs twice from dummy, but just in case ... His reward was obvious and no one could blame East. Thus, when the contract appears hopeless, with a bit of imagination you can pull the occasional rabbit out of the hat.

Remember for the future to use *the power of the closed hand.*

Before we leave this topic, let your imagination run wild on the hand
below:

Quiz

East/West Game. Dealer North.

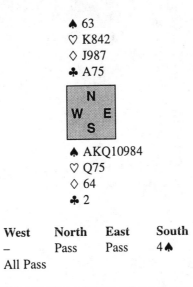

♠ 63
♡ K842
◇ J987
♣ A75

♠ AKQ10984
♡ Q75
◇ 64
♣ 2

West	North	East	South
–	Pass	Pass	4♠
All Pass			

You open 4♠ in third position at favourable vulnerability, largely to see
the whites of the opponents' eyes. Sadly, no one bites the bullet and you
are left to play at an uncomfortable level. West kicks off with ♣K, do you
have any ideas?

Unless you are fortunate in the layout of the heart suit, you will have two
losers there to go with two in diamonds. Can you find an extra chance?

Remember that the defenders know least about a hand in the first few
tricks, thereafter any 'sneaky' play is liable to come unstuck. Ideally, you
would wish to give them a headache at trick two.

Try a low heart from North. How does East possibly know that you do not
have a singleton ♡Q:

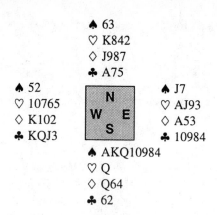

♠ 63
♥ K842
♦ J987
♣ A75

♠ 52   ♠ J7
♥ 10765   ♥ AJ93
♦ K102   ♦ A53
♣ KQJ3   ♣ 10984

♠ AKQ10984
♥ Q
♦ Q64
♣ 62

Now, failure to rise with ♡A would allow a very silly contact home. You force him to guess, and he may guess wrongly.

The alternative of crossing to ♠A and leading up to ♡K is not as good. West should know from his partner's signal if he can cash a club, whereas East has no idea.

2

HOW TO HANDLE
YOUR TRUMPS

Isn't it wonderful when we play a hand with plenty of trumps? We can demolish the enemy's token resistance and still have reserves left for other purposes. How do we deal with more meagre resources, particularly in defence? Nurture what we have, because it may produce an offspring....

We all play against them from time to time. I am referring to those amongst us who insist on slamming their cards on the table. When they believe they have just made the key decision, or winning an unexpected trick, the table can reverberate with the impact of the 'killing' play.

I always remember an old doctor friend who was one of this brigade, but sadly was also a cigar smoker. The ash at the end of his smoke would get longer and longer until he got excited about winning a trick. The card would hit the table with such a thud, closely followed by a little pile of ash.

West on the hand below was another 'slammer', and his moment of glory came at trick three:

North/South Game. Dealer North.

♠ K5
♡ J104
◇ AK52
♣ A652

♠ Q987
♡ 62
◇ 10943
♣ Q84

West	North	East	South
–	1♣	1♡	1♠
Pass	1NT	Pass	3♠
Pass	4♠	All Pass	

Defending South's 4♠ contract, he led ♡6 in response to his partner's overcall. Good news was quick to arrive, as East took the first trick with ♡K and continued with ♡A, declarer following with ♡Q.

Another heart appeared, which South ruffed with ♠J. This was West's cue to slap ♠Q on the table and look around for applause. He switched to ◇10, which ran to declarer's queen. After a trump to the king, South leant forward and said 'The rest are mine. After drawing trumps, I discard my losing club on a top diamond'.

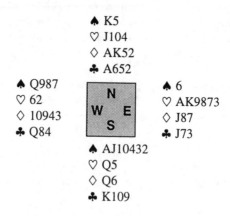

```
                    ♠ K5
                    ♡ J104
                    ◇ AK52
                    ♣ A652
 ♠ Q987                        ♠ 6
 ♡ 62         N                ♡ AK9873
 ◇ 10943   W     E             ◇ J87
 ♣ Q84        S                ♣ J73
                    ♠ AJ10432
                    ♡ Q5
                    ◇ Q6
                    ♣ K109
```

'Lucky I took my queen of spades', said West rather proudly. Suddenly he became aware of three pairs of eyes staring at him. It only remained for one of the other players to tell West what he had actually achieved. As is often the case, his partner was first to clear his throat.

'Had you discarded instead of over-ruffing, you would have won two trump tricks and defeated the contract!

Let me show you the position more clearly,' he added somewhat patronisingly.

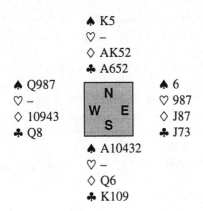

'Without prior knowledge of how the trumps divide, declarer will naturally continue with a spade to dummy's king and another spade. When he finds that East started with a singleton, it will be too late to prevent you from winning two tricks. In effect by not overruffing you have forced South to 'waste' ♠J on fresh air.

Hence, all the cards below the jack move up one on the ladder, so your ♠Q987 translates into ♠Q1098. That holding, as we know, is guaranteed to win two tricks if ♠J is on your right.'

Notice, also that if West held ♠Q876 he should still resist the temptation to overruff ♠J, just in case of:

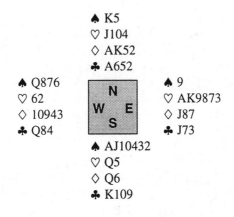

The key to knowing when to overruff is whether you hold any middle cards (8s, 9s or 10s) which might be promoted by keeping your powder dry. Had West held: ♠Q432, there would have been little point in withholding ♠Q in order to manufacture a second trump trick.

In defence, then, we need to be careful how we use our trumps. Of course, we usually find our resources are insignificant, but we still must do our best with what we have. Sometimes declarer/dummy can be over-ruffed, but as we have seen in the previous example, there are times when we must fight our instinct to claim a particular trick, in the hope of gaining two later on.

Here is another classic situation:

Love All. Dealer East.

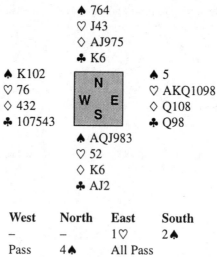

```
                    ♠ 764
                    ♡ J43
                    ◇ AJ975
                    ♣ K6
     ♠ K102                      ♠ 5
     ♡ 76          N             ♡ AKQ1098
     ◇ 432      W     E          ◇ Q108
     ♣ 107543       S            ♣ Q98
                    ♠ AQJ983
                    ♡ 52
                    ◇ K6
                    ♣ AJ2
```

West	North	East	South
–	–	1♡	2♠
Pass	4♠	All Pass	

South arrived quickly in 4♠ after East opened 1♡. West led ♡7 and his partner played three rounds of the suit, declarer ruffing with ♠Q. How should West defend?

It seems 'natural' to over-ruff with ♠K, so let us take a closer look at the trump position and see what would happen. If we use ♠K now, declarer will win our minor suit switch, and cash two top spades (♠AJ). That will draw our remaining spades (♠102) and South will make his contract. What would happen if we pitch, say, ◇2?

Twelve spades remain, distributed thus:

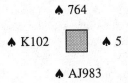

♠ 764

♠ K102 ♠ 5

♠ AJ983

Suddenly, we see that South must not only lose a trick to ♠K, but to ♠10 also. He can cross to dummy and finesse ♠J, which we take. With just ♠A to cash before our ♠10 is the highest card remaining, we have, like magic, conjured up a second trick. How did that happen?

The effect of West discarding is to negate ♠Q, or put another way, declarer has detached ♠Q from his hand, and torn it up! Play now proceeds as if she never existed.

Hence, any card below ♠Q has effectively grown in stature. No longer does West have ♠K102, it has become ♠KJ3 and that holding, as we know, provides two sure tricks when dummy has no honour.

Try this longer term venture:

North/South Game. Dealer East.

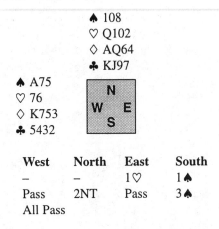

♠ 108
♡ Q102
◇ AQ64
♣ KJ97

♠ A75
♡ 76
◇ K753
♣ 5432

West	North	East	South
–	–	1♡	1♠
Pass	2NT	Pass	3♠
All Pass			

You lead ♡7 to your partner's jack. He continues with ♡A and ♡K which declarer ruffs with ♠K. Isn't it tempting to ruff with the ace? But ask yourself, what can you possibly gain by that? The ♠A is always a trick, so it doesn't matter when you take it; there is no hurry. Therefore, you discard ♣2. You never know! South leads a spade to dummy's ♠10 and one back to his jack, East producing ♠9 on the second round. Now you collect ♠A, lead a club to your partner's ace and another heart appears.

We have arrived at the following:

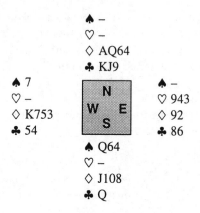

However South plays, he cannot prevent West taking a trick with ♠7. By denying yourself earlier in the play, you have received your reward.

This problem can also be rotated by 90° to reveal how careful declarer must be. Let us look at the previous deal from South's perspective. Can he thwart West's attempt to develop a second trump trick?

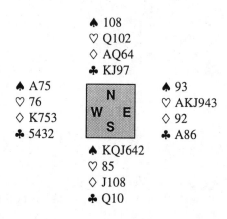

After three rounds of hearts, forcing South to ruff high, how can declarer avoid a second trump loser? The answer is to knock out East's entry to the long hearts whilst still retaining the trumps in dummy.

Thus, lead ♣Q and a second club to the king if East ducks. Another heart now cannot damage South's trump holding, as ♠108 are still intact. Without the ability to 'promote' a second trump winner, the defence is impotent.

Treading gingerly applies with even more force if you started with less than the usual eight-card fit. How would you manage 4♡ on these cards?

East/West Game. Dealer South.

```
              ♠ A542
              ♡ 54
              ◇ 65
              ♣ AJ982
              ┌─────────┐
              │    N    │
              │  W   E  │
              │    S    │
              └─────────┘
              ♠ Q63
              ♡ AKJ108
              ◇ 7
              ♣ KQ104
```

West	North	East	South
–	–	–	1♡
2◇	Dble(i)	3◇	3♡ (ii)
Pass	4♡	All Pass	

(i) A 'negative double', showing four spades and at least seven points.

(ii) 4♣ might have been better.

The defence begin with two top diamonds, forcing declarer to ruff. Let us follow an orthodox line of play. South cashes ♡A, crosses to ♣A and finesses ♡10. However, West wins ♡Q and presses on with diamonds. After ruffing, declarer lays down ♡ K but the suit fails to divide and he is vanquished.

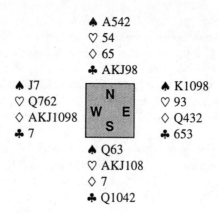

```
                    ♠ A542
                    ♡ 54
                    ◇ 65
                    ♣ AKJ98
        ♠ J7          N        ♠ K1098
        ♡ Q762                 ♡ 93
        ◇ AKJ1098  W     E     ◇ Q432
        ♣ 7          S        ♣ 653
                    ♠ Q63
                    ♡ AKJ108
                    ◇ 7
                    ♣ Q1042
```

Let us replay the hand, bearing in mind the need for tight control of trumps.

At trick three, declarer leads out ♡J, not minding who wins. With a trump still left in dummy, the defence cannot usefully continue diamonds and any other play will result in an easy ten tricks (five clubs, four hearts and ♠A). Should West play low, South can cash ♡AK, and then switch his attention to clubs.

So whether declarer or defender, handle your trumps with care!

3
GOOD HAND, SHAME ABOUT THE RESULT!

We greet the appearance of a really exciting hand as if it were a long-lost friend. Clearly the time has come to get that much-needed slam, or to pick up a juicy penalty. However, it never ceases to amaze me how often it all ends in tears ....

Rewarding as playing bridge undoubtedly is, it does have certain frustrations and low points. Heading the list for me is the following scenario.

Having gone most of the evening picking up no 'cards' whatsoever, and (in my case, at least) getting increasingly grumpy about it, you are delighted to finally welcome something worth talking about. Expecting to recoup some of those earlier losses, what happens? Instead of gaining a hefty plus score, you finish up adding to the ever-mounting debt. Why does this happen?!

Take West's rousing collection, and look at what happened to him:

North/South Game. Dealer North.

$$\spadesuit \text{ AK9}$$
$$\heartsuit \text{ A97}$$
$$\diamondsuit \text{ } -$$
$$\clubsuit \text{ AKQJ987}$$

West	North	East	South
–	Pass	Pass	1 ◇
Dble	1 ♠	Pass	2 ♡
4 ♣	4 ◇	Pass	5 ◇
Dble	All Pass		

Your vulnerable opponents appear to have lost their collective minds. Looking at more than half the deck, and three aces to boot, it is time to improve your bank balance. Sad to relate, this is the whole hand:

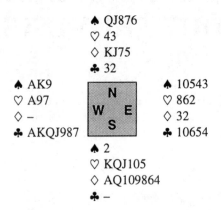

```
                    ♠ QJ876
                    ♡ 43
                    ◇ KJ75
                    ♣ 32
      ♠ AK9          N          ♠ 10543
      ♡ A97                     ♡ 862
      ◇ -       W       E       ◇ 32
      ♣ AKQJ987      S          ♣ 10654
                    ♠ 2
                    ♡ KQJ105
                    ◇ AQ109864
                    ♣ -
```

You lead ♣A, but that is ruffed. A bad start. Trumps are quickly drawn and South tries a sneaky ♡10 from hand. You grab ♡A and attempt to cash the top spades, but no luck there either. The last chance is that East will have ♡K, but it is not to be.

I blame East, in fact: how can he hold such a lousy hand *now*. Why couldn't he wait a couple of deals? It is hard to believe that the best result West can achieve is to sacrifice in 6♣, at a net cost of 200 points (two down doubled less 100 honours).

Sometimes a helpful opponent saves you from a cruel fate. Note West's contribution on the next deal:

East/West Game. Dealer West.

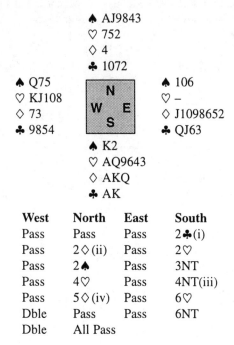

♠ AJ9843
♡ 752
◊ 4
♣ 1072

♠ Q75
♡ KJ108
◊ 73
♣ 9854

♠ 106
♡ –
◊ J1098652
♣ QJ63

♠ K2
♡ AQ9643
◊ AKQ
♣ AK

West	North	East	South
Pass	Pass	Pass	2♣(i)
Pass	2◊ (ii)	Pass	2♡
Pass	2♠	Pass	3NT
Pass	4♡	Pass	4NT(iii)
Pass	5◊ (iv)	Pass	6♡
Dble	Pass	Pass	6NT
Dble	All Pass		

(i)   Forcing to game
(ii)   Negative
(iii) Blackwood
(iv) One ace

North/South had a reasonable sequence, but arrived in a slam which was doomed due to the bad trump break. South was destined to have the usual awful result with a great hand, but what happened? West got greedy and doubled 6♡. In one respect he was right, 6♡ was indeed going down, but in a more important respect he was completely wrong. He had no defence to 6♠ or 6NT and his double of the latter was more in pique than a measure of confidence in the outcome.

Declarer won the opening club lead, cashed ♠K and led a spade to the jack. When the finesse worked and East followed suit, he had twelve tricks. In the end, with some assistance from the westerly quarter, South's super hand had gained its just desserts, as it was meant to.

So, experience tells us that we should not be greedy, because that greed often causes our downfall. It is still easy to get carried away, in more ways than one, when we view a vast array of aces and kings. Feast your eyes on this collection:

Game All. Dealer South.

♠ A63
♡ A
◇ AKJ7
♣ AKQ84

Sitting South, as dealer, you open 2♣ (your strongest bid) and hear a positive reply of 2♡. Now it's off to the races. You continue with 3♣ and partner repeats his hearts. Time for Blackwood, and the auction proceeds as follows:

North	South
–	2♣
2♡	3♣
3♡	4NT(i)
5♣	5NT(ii)
6◇	6NT
Pass	

(i)   Blackwood for aces
(ii) Blackwood for kings (6◇ shows one)

The response of 6◇ was disappointing, but surely 6NT would be safe? West leads ♡4 and dummy goes down:

♠ Q942
♡ KQJ1085
◊ 62
♣ 3

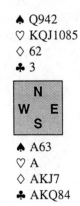

♠ A63
♡ A
◊ AKJ7
♣ AKQ84

All those lovely heart tricks over there, but only one way to reach them. With a sinking feeling, you win ♡A, cash ♠A and follow with a spade towards the queen. Sad to relate, East has ♠K and when clubs divide 5-2 you are defeated by *five* tricks. Humiliation that even 150 for honours fails to alleviate.

Let's have another hand, shall we?

Dealer South.

♠ AKJ97
♡ AQ1042
◊ AKJ
♣ –

Here is the whole auction:

North	South
–	2♣
2◊ (i)	2♠
2NT(ii)	3♡
3♠	4♣ (iii)
4♠	Pass

(i)   A negative response usually less than one and a half quick tricks

(ii) A double negative, less than five points

(iii) Cuebid, still trying for a slam

Our sights have lowered and lowered as the sequence developed, and now we have the apparently modest task of collecting ten tricks. However ....

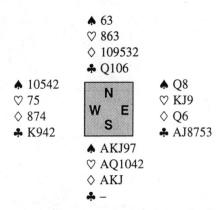

```
                    ♠ 63
                    ♡ 863
                    ◇ 109532
                    ♣ Q106
     ♠ 10542          N          ♠ Q8
     ♡ 75                        ♡ KJ9
     ◇ 874         W     E       ◇ Q6
     ♣ K942           S          ♣ AJ8753
                    ♠ AKJ97
                    ♡ AQ1042
                    ◇ AKJ
                    ♣ –
```

West leads ♣2 to the ten, jack and ♠7. Already feeling slightly uncomfortable about the shortage of trumps, you try ♡A and another heart. East collects ♡J and another club appears, forcing you to ruff again.

You cash ♠AK, noting that the queen falls, draw one further trump and try ◇AK. Once more the queen comes tumbling down, so you take the jack, but it is only the ninth trick. Out of ideas, you have to concede defeat. Despite an accommodating layout of the cards, you still have to open your wallet!

The plot was lost during the bidding. Over 3♠, you should try 4♡, showing at least five cards in the suit and enabling North to select his preferred major. The extra trump is all-important here, and 4♡ would be an easy ride in practice.

A more circumspect approach would have reaped a rich reward on the previous hand too. Instead of rushing into 6NT, South should choose 6♡ over 6◇, because he cannot guarantee reaching dummy. Partner has bid and re-bid hearts, so a singleton ace is adequate support. Even 7♡ would have been easy.

It is all too common that the anticipation of great things to come causes us to reach too high. It is worth remembering the next time you are lucky enough to hold a 2♣ opener, that big hands often produce small results. *Make sure of your plus.*

With that phrase indelibly printed on your mind, see what you make of these (you are West):

1. Love All. Dealer West.

♠ A64
♡ AKQJ86
◊ A97
♣ A

West	East
2♣	2◊
2♡	3♡
?	

2. Game All. Dealer West.

♠ KQJ10875
♡ 74
◊ AK
♣ AK

West	East
2♣	2◊
2♠	3♣
3♠	4♣
?	

Rarely, if ever, has there been a quiz where you hold wonderful hands, but can you find the best route to a solid plus score? Let's find out.

1. Your best shot is 3NT. With nine tricks guaranteed, this action satisfies the 'safety first' criterion. Should East have something extra, it also leaves room for him to show it without committing the partnership to the five level. In case you imagined that 4♡ was 100% secure, what if this was your dummy?

♠ A64	N	♠ J75
♡ AKQJ86	W E	♡ 10932
◊ A97	S	◊ J64
♣ A		♣ Q108

Where is your tenth trick?

2. Were you tempted to go for a 4◊ cuebid, or even Blackwood? I hope not, because this hand is not as good as it looks! In fact I would opt for an 'old woman's' 4♠ bid. Let me explain why.

We have to examine what is needed to make a slam into a *good* proposition. Surely ♡A and seven reasonable clubs would suffice, well ....

♠ KQJ10875	N	♠ 6
♡ 74	W E	♡ A8
◊ AK	S	◊ J7
♣ AK		♣ Q9865432

Both 6♣ and 6♠ are down on a heart lead. That is assuming East holds the 'perfect' hand. Opposite moderate collections, even 5♣ could need a following wind:

♠ KQJ10875	N	♠ 6
♡ 74	W E	♡ Q8
◊ AK	S	◊ J75
♣ AK		♣ Q986543

Once again, the long term winner is the cautious 'bank the money' route.

4
CONVENTIONS, DO WE NEED THEM?

To play chess effectively, one needs to be abreast of the latest 'opening theory'. I was always too lazy to worry about what Anonkov and Bloggsov had played last week in Outer Mongolia. If I was *that* interested in studying minutiae, I would have been a solicitor!

No, bridge offered the free open spaces where one can express oneself with flair and imagination, rather than via hard-learnt rules. However, as the years have gone by, the convention-hungry have taken over. Thus each sequence known to man now has a possible added dimension. Look at this effort by Meckstroth and Rodwell.

First imagine what this would mean at the local club, and then read their interpretation:

West	East
1♣(i)	2◇(ii)
3♣(iii)	3♠(iv)
4◇(v)	4NT(vi)
5♣(vii)	5◇(viii)
6♠(ix)	Pass

(i)   16+ points, the Precision Club
(ii)   5+ *hearts,* 9 or more points
(iii)   Shows heart support and at least five controls (ace = 2, king = 1)
(iv)   Natural – hooray!
(v)   Roman Key Card Blackwood in *spades*
(vi)   Two out of the five 'aces' (4 aces and ♠K)
(vii)   Do you have ♠Q?
(viii) No!
(ix)   End of story

These were the two hands:

West		East
♠ AJ94		♠ K876
♡ K75		♡ AJ1064
◇ AKJ92		◇ 82
♣ A		♣ Q6

Very nice, I am sure, but you do rather long for the natural auction, for example:

West	East
1◇	1♡
2♠	4♠
6♠	Pass

If bridge is to become a spectator sport, the latter approach is the way to go. It is faster, and more crucially, the viewing public can follow what is going on.

But should we use any conventions at all? The old die-hards can help, for others we should stick to the following rules:

1. They *must* be easy to remember.
2. They should provide valuable information.
3. They should not displace an essential *natural* bid.

If you analyse the conventions which have stood the test of time e.g. Stayman or Blackwood (Gerber), you will readily see that they conform to all three tests. A 'new kid on the block' is the '*splinter*' bid, and it is one which I would heartily recommend you adopt.

First, what is a splinter bid? Over an opening 1♡ or 1♠, a double jump response of 4♣ or 4◇ shows a hand which has the values to raise partner to game, with a singleton in the suit chosen. For example with:

♠ QJ853
♡ A108
◇ A732
♣ 8

you respond 4♣ if your partner opens 1♠ or with:

> ♠ AQ73
> ♡ Q1084
> ◇ KJ92
> ♣ 7

you would bid 4♣ if partner opened 1♡ or 1♠. Before I continue, what would you bid with these hands in reply to a 1♡ opening?

(a)	♠ AQ4	(b)	♠ A853	(c)	♠ K108
	♡ KJ108		♡ KJ93		♡ J842
	◇ 7		◇ 7		◇ AK1094
	♣ Q10842		♣ Q842		♣ 8

My suggestions would be:

(a) 4◇ The classic splinter bid.
(b) 3♡ You are not quite worth a splinter, although it is sorely tempting. As with all conventions if we overuse them, they are less effective.
(c) 4♣ A good test of whether a hand justifies a splinter bid is whether you would open it in third chair. Here I would, so I select 4♣. Note that, if you decide a hand is worth a raise to game, there is no difference in strength between 4♣ (splinter) and a direct 4♡. If you choose the latter, you should not have a singleton *and* a decent hand.

To see how useful this convention can be, here are a couple of example hands (North is the dealer):

> ♠ KQ1084
> ♡ A73
> ◇ KJ
> ♣ 543

```
      N
  W       E
      S
```

> ♠ A975
> ♡ KQ42
> ◇ A753
> ♣ 6

North	South
1♠	4♣(i)
4NT(ii)	5♡(iii)
6♠	Pass

(i)   Splinter bid
(ii)   Blackwood
(iii) Two aces

Even though North has a minimum opener, he can immediately identify that there is no 'wastage'. His partner's splinter has hit the perfect spot. Every honour card is working, so all he needs for a slam is South to have two aces.

On the other side of the coin:

♠ Q73
♡ AQJ94
♢ Q6
♣ KJ9

♠ A964
♡ K1083
♢ AJ43
♣ 6

North	South
1♡	4♣
4♡	Pass

This time, North has 15 points, but the club strength is completely wasted. With two queens in the key suits (diamonds and spades), it is almost certain there will be at least one loser somewhere, to go with ♣A. North can sign off in 4♡, confident that a slam is highly unlikely.

Remember that the hand which employs a splinter bid should have 11-13 points. This is because there is little room left for investigation after a 4♣/♢ response, so the opener needs to be confident that partner will not have either:

1. Extra strength e.g.

♠ Q73
♡ AQJ94
◊ Q6
♣ KJ9

♠ AKJ4
♡ K1083
◊ A743
♣ 6

which could result in a good slam being missed on our second hand or:

2. Be too weak:

♠ KQ1084
♡ A73
◊ KJ
♣ 543

♠ A975
♡ Q642
◊ A753
♣ 6

which might result in a hopeless slam being reached on our first hand.

Finally, two examples to remind you of the principle:

Dealer North.

♠ Q10842
♡ A43
◊ A652
♣ Q

♠ AK73
♡ K1085
◊ 8
♣ J1073

North	South
1♠	4◊(i)
4♠	Pass

(i)   A splinter bid; a raise to 4♠ and a singleton diamond.

Even though North has the perfect holding in diamonds, having just the ace, he is so minimum that he can do no more than sign-off in 4♠.

♠ KQ842
♡ Q6
◊ AQ4
♣ A73

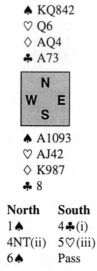

♠ A1093
♡ AJ42
◊ K987
♣ 8

North	South
1♠	4♣(i)
4NT(ii)	5♡(iii)
6♠	Pass

(i) Splinter bid   (ii) Blackwood   (iii) Two aces

This time North was close to looking for a grand slam, and could have checked if South held two kings via 5NT. However, he knew that possession of two aces and two kings is outside the range for a 'splinter' (11-13 points), so he wisely settled for 6♠.

I firmly believe that this convention will be with us for a long time. It is easy to use, an excellent aid to constructive bidding, and does not usurp the meaning of an otherwise valuable bid. When was the last time that you responded 4♣ or 4♦ (natural and pre-emptive) to an opening 1♡ or 1♠? I would suggest that you probably can't remember. This convention does not adversely affect everyday auctions, and that is vitally important.

Splinters can be extended to other sequences, let us examine how these hands could be bid:

> ♠ KQ842
> ♡ A1096
> ◇ AJ4
> ♣ 8

```
      N
   W     E
      S
```

> ♠ A10
> ♡ KQ843
> ◇ K65
> ♣ 432

North	South
1♠	2♡
4♣(i)	4NT(ii)
5♡(iii)	6♡
Pass	

(i)   Splinter
(ii) Blackwood
(iii) Two aces

Rather than just raising 2♡ to 4♡, North employs our new found tool. By bidding 4♣ he can pinpoint the singleton club, as well as show the values for game. South can accurately judge how the hands fit together. With an above-minimum 2♡ response, plus no wastage in clubs, he embarks on a slam-hunt. Blackwood confirms the possession of enough aces, and there they are.

Alternatively:

♠ KQ842
♡ A1096
◊ AJ4
♣ 8

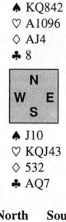

♠ J10
♡ KQJ43
◊ 532
♣ AQ7

North	South
1♠	2♡
4♣(i)	4♡
Pass	

(i)   Splinter

Here, South can see that he has weakness in diamonds, so he quietly signs off in game, despite having a nearly identical hand to the previous example. It is not simply a matter of 'how much', but 'where'.

There are more sophisticated 'splinters' available, and for those who wish to extend their armoury, remember the following rule for ease of application.

If a player makes a jump bid in a suit, when a non-jump bid would have been forcing, then the call is a splinter. So:

1♠ – 2♡ – 4◊   is a splinter because 3◊ is forcing; but
1♡ – 1♠ – 3♣   is natural because 2♣ is not forcing.

However, I firmly recommend that you stick to the basic splinter first, and see how you like it. Good Luck!

Another slam convention worth its weight in paper is *Blackwood*. Invented by the great American player, Easley Blackwood, it uses 4NT as a request for partner to show the number of aces he holds. He does this by bidding 5♣ with zero (or exceptionally four), 5♦ with one, 5♡ with two and 5♠ with three. I believe its longevity is a function of the following:

1. It is easy to apply and thus to remember.
2. The bid of 4NT is not often used or needed for other meanings.
3. It locates a valuable piece of information.

However, because of the above it does have a tendency to be over-used or misused. The person employing the convention should *know* what to do when they hear the reply. It is the last piece of the jigsaw. Take this situation:

♠ KQJ94
♡ AK73
♦ Q4
♣ A7

West	North	East	South
1♠	Pass	3♠	Pass
?			

It is quite feasible that 6♠ is a good contract and equally possible that it is not. If we use Blackwood now, the answer will not necessarily tell us anything. For example, a 5♦ reply showing one ace does not advance our cause at all. East could have either:

♠ A10652
♡ 65
♦ K73
♣ K84

where 6♠ is easy; or

♠ A1065
♡ J65
♦ K7
♣ QJ65

where it is almost hopeless.

Here, West must cuebid 4♣ and develop the hand more slowly. If East signs-off with 4♠, he can leave matters well alone, but if he bids 4◇ (showing ◇ A or possibly ◇ K *and* a reasonable hand), it is sensible to use Blackwood.

The 4NT bidder takes control of the auction and responder must respect any decision made. A fine example of this principle came from a hand sent in by Rear Admiral John Ievers of Lymington. His partner picked up the following impressive collection:

♠ AKJ9876
♡ –
◇ 6
♣ KQJ74

First in hand, vulnerable against not, she opened 2♠.

This is how the auction developed:

West	North	East	South
–	–	–	2♠
Pass	4NT(i)	Pass	5◇(ii)
Pass	6♡	Pass	?

(i)   Blackwood
(ii)   One ace

Partner's leap to 6♡ was a distinct turn for the worse, and it was extremely tempting to retreat to the 'security' of 6♠. Nevertheless, she had not been asked to bid and so, bravely in my view, elected to pass 6♡, which became the final contract. East led ♣ A and she tabled her dummy.

This was the full deal:

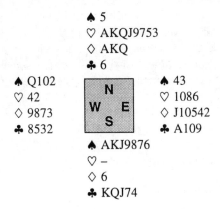

```
                  ♠ 5
                  ♡ AKQJ9753
                  ◇ AKQ
                  ♣ 6
    ♠ Q102          N        ♠ 43
    ♡ 42                     ♡ 1086
    ◇ 9873      W       E    ◇ J10542
    ♣ 8532         S         ♣ A109
                  ♠ AKJ9876
                  ♡ –
                  ◇ 6
                  ♣ KQJ74
```

Somewhat nervous that the combination of a heart void and a minimum point count for her Acol 2♠ opener might not be all that the doctor ordered, she was delighted to hear a warm 'Thank you, partner' from a Northerly direction.

The play was soon over with declarer winning East's diamond switch at trick two, painlessly drawing trumps and claiming the balance. South's confidence in her partner had been amply rewarded.

Blackwood has saved me from many a hopeless slam over the years and will no doubt continue to do so in the future. It has become one of the foundations of the modern game, and along with 'Stayman', also named after its American inventor, I am sure it will be with us for years to come.

Can you take on the world using only Blackwood, Stayman and Splinters? Well, Andrew Robson and I managed with little else for five years with reasonable success. Of course, less system puts more of the focus on partnership understanding and individual judgement; it also adds to our fun!

As a final warning to the convention-happy, here is a story of Zia Mahmood and I at the 1995 Cavendish Tournament in New York ....

It is a scenario which must have occurred a million times. A bridge player is asked by another to have a game, they agree not to employ too many gadgets and just 'have a laugh'. Everything goes wonderfully well, so they agree to a second encounter and lo and behold the same thing happens. Is this person the answer to all their bridge prayers?

Soon, stage two takes over; they decide to play on a 'regular basis'. These words signal the end of their honeymoon period, and move the partnership into a downhill spiral. Maybe they will emerge some time later and survive the trials and tribulations of their 'system', but equally likely they will not.

I write these words having just played with Zia Mahmood in The Cavendish. This event marked the transformation of our partnership from 'occasional' to 'regular'. Just look at the kind of thing which happened:

Love All. Dealer South.

```
            ♠ 87432
            ♡ 7
            ◊ J943
            ♣ Q62
            ┌─────────┐
            │    N    │
            │  W   E  │
            │    S    │
            └─────────┘
            ♠ AKQ95
            ♡ AKQ
            ◊ AQ10
            ♣ J10
```

West	North	East	South
–	–	–	2♣(i)
Pass	2♡(ii)	Pass	2♠
Pass	3♠	Pass	3NT(iii)
Pass	4♡	Pass	4♠
Pass	5♣	Pass	6♡
Pass	6♠	All Pass	

(i)   Strong opening, forcing to game
(ii) A 'double negative' 0-3 points
(iii) See below

A confused sequence where neither of us had a clue what was going on, and all because of our system 'agreements'. To explain more fully, South felt his 3NT bid was natural but North knew that the partnership had discussed this sort of situation, and had agreed that 3NT would be a 'general slam try'.

South nearly passed North's 4♡(!), because he thought it was natural, but, having avoided that obstacle, leapt to 6♡ over North's 5♣ cuebid. Are you lost, because the two of us certainly were. In the end we reached a totally hopeless slam which I would like to think would not have happened without our 'helpful' gadgets.

Before we leave this deal, just imagine that you are playing in the more normal contract of 4♠ and West leads ♣A and another club to East's king. At trick three a third round of clubs follows and you ...? With a discard being of no help to you, it seems reasonable to ruff high to avoid West scoring an easy ruff. Have I persuaded you into the losing line?

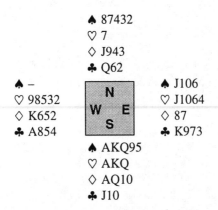

```
              ♠ 87432
              ♡ 7
              ◇ J943
              ♣ Q62
♠ -                         ♠ J106
♡ 98532        N            ♡ J1064
◇ K652      W     E         ◇ 87
♣ A854         S            ♣ K973
              ♠ AKQ95
              ♡ AKQ
              ◇ AQ10
              ♣ J10
```

After wasting your ♠Q, cashing ♠A and later taking a diamond finesse you will emerge, less than triumphant, with nine tricks. West did actually defend that way against 6♠ so Zia was three down, but whether he would have found the same inspired lead against 4♠, we shall never know.

As to Zia and myself, only time will tell whether this was our swan-song or if we have a rosy future. Two years on, my vote is for the former!

5
TRIPPING THE HIGH WIRE

When I used to play tennis, it was an easy task to diagnose a weakness. Any ball coming within the vicinity of my backhand sent a message of fear to the brain and paralysis to the muscles. Embarrassment invariably followed.

At bridge, however, it is not always so easy to spot where one needs to improve. With very few exceptions, Raymond Brock being one that comes to mind, the area of high-level competition appears to catch us all out....

When to sacrifice, when to double or bid 'one for the road', or even that rare commodity nowadays – when to 'Pass'.

The stakes are high, so a wrong decision will inevitably be costly. Here are a couple of problems, which occurred on consecutive hands, see what you think (you are North):

1. East/West Game. Dealer North.

♠ 53	West	North	East	South
♡ AKQ	–	1♢	Pass	3♢
♢ 1097653	Dble	Pass	4♠	Pass
♣ K4	Pass	?		

2. North/South Game. Dealer East.

♠ K106	West	North	East	South
♡ A1094	–	–	Pass	1♠
♢ A106	2♢	Dble(i)	3♢	4♡
♣ 753	5♢	?		

    (i)   Showing four hearts and at least 8 points

On the first, you are faced with a choice of whether to sacrifice in 5◊ or defend 4♠. On the second, do you double the opponents' 5◊ sacrifice or, fearing a poor return, bid 5♠ ? Place your bets, please, before we see the whole picture.

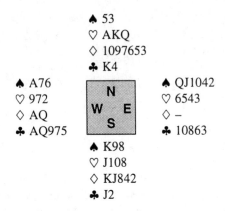

At the table, North elected to bid 5◊, which West gratefully doubled. There was no way to avoid five losers (two spades, two diamonds and a club) so North/South conceded 500 points. This would have netted a small profit if 4♠ was going to succeed, but was it?

In 4♠, on a diamond lead, East could insert ◊Q, cash ◊A pitching two hearts and eventually come to hand with a heart ruff to take the spade finesse. A bit hairy, but nevertheless a route to 620 points. So was North right in bidding 5♡?

In my view the answer is 'no', but the root cause of North's dilemma arose on the previous round of the auction. He was justifiably concerned that a diamond lead would be fatal for the defence in 4♠, and should have sought to reduce that risk by bidding 3♡ over West's double. He could then safely pass 4♠, expecting a heart lead.

On the very next board, North again erred in judgement:

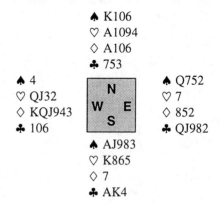

East/West bid 5◇ as a sacrifice over 4♡. This should have resulted in North doubling them. After a trump lead, the usual start against a sacrifice bid, accurate defence would beat the contract by six tricks and net a massive 1400 points. Instead North elected to continue with 5♡, which even had it made, would only score 650 points.

However, worse news was to follow. When West led ◇K, South took the ace and continued with ♡A and another heart from dummy. He believed that West must be short in hearts for his 5◇ call, but he was wrong. When East showed out on the second heart, it was too late to recover. Not only did North/South miss winning the lottery, but they had the ignominy of going down at the five level.

I am sure North's misjudgement on the first hand affected his view of the second. A warning for all bridge players.

How about, 'When in doubt, bid one more'? Of course, if everyone constantly 'bid one more', competitive sequences would finish at the seven level! No, the idea behind the saying is that, when you are faced with a marginal decision as to whether to play or defend, then one should play.

To see why this advice has stood the test of time, witness the deal below, played in a match between Sweden and the Netherlands – two of Europe's strongest bridge nations.

North/South Game. Dealer East.

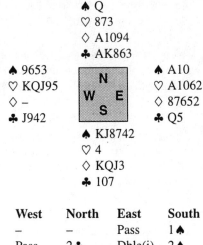

	♠ Q	
	♡ 873	
	◇ A1094	
	♣ AK863	
♠ 9653		♠ A10
♡ KQJ95		♡ A1062
◇ –		◇ 87652
♣ J942		♣ Q5
	♠ KJ8742	
	♡ 4	
	◇ KQJ3	
	♣ 107	

West	North	East	South
–	–	Pass	1♠
Pass	2♣	Dble(i)	2♠
4♡	Dble	All Pass	

(i)   For takeout

With the Netherlands East/West, the sequence took a rather unexpected turn, particularly from North's point of view. After his partner opened the bidding with 1♠, he could hardly have expected to defend a contract of 4♡ doubled. No doubt he was anticipating a large penalty, but he was soon to be disillusioned. He led a top club and switched accurately enough to a trump.

Declarer won in hand and continued with a second club. Again, North won to continue trumps, but to no avail. West won cheaply and cashed two club tricks, pitching a spade and a diamond from dummy. A spade to the ace was followed by a diamond ruff and West could now deal with two of his losing spades by ruffing in dummy.

In all, West collected seven trump tricks, two clubs and ♠A to make his contract. Note that, if North starts with a trump lead, and continues trumps at every turn, 4♡ would be defeated by one trick. It is rarely wrong to defend in this way when your side has the balance of strength.

Over at another table, the Dutch were North/South. This is what happened:

West	North	East	South
–	–	1♦	1♠
2♥	3♣	3♥	3♠
4♥	4♠	All Pass	

Here, North judged to continue on to 4♠ rather than seek a penalty from 4♥, despite holding a singleton ♠Q. In passing, look at East's opening bid, a balanced ten points with an abysmal suit. Whatever next?

West was anxious to collect his diamond ruffs, so he sought to alert his partner to that by making an unusual lead. He chose ♥J, theoretically showing the ten. As East held ♥10 himself, one would have thought that the message would get through, but I'm afraid not. East woodenly won ♥A and led a heart back.

Declarer ruffed and led a spade to the queen, which East might have ducked with some profit, but he continued with his feeble defence, by winning ♠A and leading a third heart. South ruffed, drew two top trumps, leaving West with ♠9 and led minor suit winners. The defence could take its trump trick whenever it wished.

Once more, the technically losing decision of North to bid 4♠ was proved to be a winner in practice. The biggest single reason for 'bidding one more' is that the defence often take one less!

As always in bridge, there is the other side of the coin, which I would call 'Antique Syndrome' ….

My wife and I deny ourselves the pleasure of visiting auctions. Why, you might well ask, when we both like antiques and adore hunting for 'bargains'? Self-control, or the lack of it to be more precise, is the rather shameful answer.

There is a discipline required when you see a vase or clock you really fancy. A little man inside you should be saying 'Do not go beyond your budget', but somehow he cannot be heard over the auctioneer's constant patter. Higher and higher we go, caught up in the excitement of the moment.

Bridge players, however expert they may be, can fall into the same trap, 'I will *not* be outbid'. Look at this hand from the 1996 Premier League.

North/South Game. Dealer North.

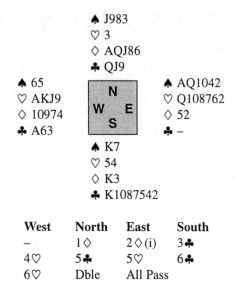

	♠ J983		
	♡ 3		
	◊ AQJ86		
	♣ QJ9		

♠ 65
♡ AKJ9
◊ 10974
♣ A63

♠ AQ1042
♡ Q108762
◊ 52
♣ –

♠ K7
♡ 54
◊ K3
♣ K1087542

West	North	East	South
–	1◊	2◊(i)	3♣
4♡	5♣	5♡	6♣
6♡	Dble	All Pass	

(i)   Michaels cuebid, showing at least 5-5 in the major suits.

On view were four of our finest. North/South were John Armstrong and Graham Kirby, and sitting East/West were Phillip King and Les Steel. The auction had a surreal look to it. Despite being vulnerable and holding just twenty points between them, North/South seemed happy to attempt a slam, which if doubled would cost a comfortable 500 points. No, their opponents apparently did not believe that 'aces win tricks'. They went on to 6♡ – maybe they felt that Kirby could walk on water.

Notice that no one missed their turn, including North's heroic 5♣ call. Who cares that he held 11 points and had already opened the bidding?

North did not fancy cashing ◊A, so he tried ♣Q instead. Away went one of the diamond losers. Declarer drew trumps and led a spade. He only required North to hold ♠K and he was home. And why shouldn't he, after all he had opened the bidding. Sadly there was no happy ending.

So there we have it. The reason why it is tough to judge the winning action in high level competitive auctions is that no hard and fast rule exists. That's my excuse anyway!

6
WEAK OR STRONG 1NT?

When I was a young player, which seems rather a long time ago now, I rapidly became disillusioned with the all-conquering weak no trump opener. It seemed to be incurring vast penalties on a fairly frequent basis, and appeared to have little logic to its use. After all a 4-3-3-3 12-point hand is hardly one to send us into raptures, and yet we deny ourselves the option of safely playing in a one-level suit contract. We put our heads above the parapet at the exact time when we should be keeping low.

Here is the sort of thing which was happening to me:

Game All. Dealer South.

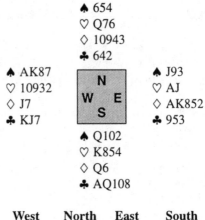

```
                    ♠ 654
                    ♡ Q76
                    ◇ 10943
                    ♣ 642
     ♠ AK87                        ♠ J93
     ♡ 10932          N            ♡ AJ
     ◇ J7          W     E         ◇ AK852
     ♣ KJ7            S            ♣ 953
                    ♠ Q102
                    ♡ K854
                    ◇ Q6
                    ♣ AQ108
```

West	North	East	South
–	–	–	1NT(i)
Pass	Pass	Dble	Pass
Pass	Rdbl(ii)	Pass	2♣
Dble	All Pass		

(i)   12-14 points
(ii) For rescue!

South opened an immaculate example of the weak 1NT. He would have survived and shown a profit (because East/West can make 3NT), until East found a hair-trigger double. The odds were strongly on his side as West could hold up to 14 points whereas North should not have more than 10.

The resultant carnage was made worse by the curious propensity of weak no trumpers to bail out at any price, showing a marked lack of faith in their beloved. What excuse North had for re-doubling, I do not know, but with a totally balanced hand, he sought to find a suit contract. Doesn't suit you, sir!

This East/West pair were not going to let their enemy off the hook, and proceeded to double at the first opportunity. When you have the opposition on the run, don't let them get away.

The defenders had great fun. West led ♠A and switched to ♡10 which ran to declarer's ♡K. With nothing better to do, South returned a heart, ducked to East's ace. The play had started well, but now ....

East cashed ◇AK and led a third round, ruffed by West with ♣7 whilst declarer pitched a spade. The ♠K was taken before a heart appeared, ruffed by East, who pressed on with diamonds. South should have thrown a heart, but he tried ♣Q, anxious to obtain the lead. West over-ruffed and played a heart for East to ruff.

The final ignominy came when East led his last diamond and South could not prevent West from making ♣J. A mere 1400 points.

Despite the above, I would not be able to move under the weight of correspondence, if I didn't show the other side of the coin:

East/West Game. Dealer South.

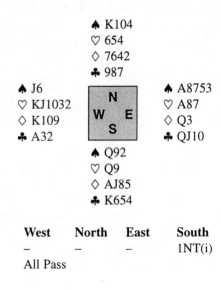

♠ K104
♡ 654
◇ 7642
♣ 987

♠ J6
♡ KJ1032
◇ K109
♣ A32

♠ A8753
♡ A87
◇ Q3
♣ QJ10

♠ Q92
♡ Q9
◇ AJ85
♣ K654

West	North	East	South
–	–	–	1NT(i)
All Pass			

(i)   12-14

South's weak 1NT strikes! The opponents can make a vulnerable game, and yet neither feels comfortable in competing.

One simply cannot afford to be timid where the weak no-trump is concerned. Compete or die. Here East should bid 2♠ or double. West could be excused because he sat in the 'exposed' seat, i.e. he did not know that North held a weakish hand.

Of course, there are risks involved when you act in marginal situations, but one stands to lose a great deal by being over-cautious.

Having lambasted the weak 1NT opening, it would be unfair of me not to give the counter-arguments, and who better to do that than the late Victor Mollo, bridge writer par excellence.

> *'The opening 1NT is by far the best bid there is, describing in one go, strength and shape within narrow limits, a process which would otherwise require two or three rounds of bidding. It follows that the more often you can bid 1NT the better, and since hands in*

the 12-14 range come up more frequently than those in the 15-17 or 16-18 brackets, the weak no trump is a priori superior to the strong.

More games are played in 3NT than any other, and the best way for declarer to get there is by a direct 1NT – 3NT sequence. No suit having been mentioned, the opponents lead in the dark and are less likely to find a killing defence. here again, the frequency factor works for the weak no trump.

As soon as a player has bid 1NT, partner knows, and no one else does, to whom the hand belongs and how far it is safe to go. Opponents must guess, speculate and take chances. If they err on the side of caution, they may miss a partial or even a game. If they step in when they are outgunned, they risk incurring a penalty.

In this context, the weak no trump is always a challenge, creating tension and putting pressure on the other side.

By contrast, the strong no trump presents no challenge and is rather a signal to relax. Knowing that opener holds nearly half the high-card strength of the pack, opponents have little temptation to contest the auction. With more to lose on the swings than to gain on the roundabouts, it is always safe to pass on a balanced hand.

One of the drawbacks of the strong no trump is that it poses no problems for opponents. It is easy for them to do the right thing for most of the time, it simply means do nothing.

With so much going for it, how is it that everyone hasn't long ago converted to the weak no trump? The answer lies in the fear of being doubled and penalised, especially at unfavourable vulnerability.

The double of 1NT is primarily for penalties. Partner will leave it on the slightest provocation and, of course, it can cost 800 or more. In practice, this very seldom happens. For one thing, opener's partner will have a suit of more than four cards two thirds of the time. Once in seven deals he will have a six-card suit. he needn't stick the double. Even on a completely balanced hand he can often wriggle out of trouble by bidding his shortest suit *and following it up with an SOS redouble. At worst, a 4-3 Moysian fit will provide a refuge from the storm.*

I have played the weak no trump, regardless of vulnerability, for some fifty years. The occasional penalty – and there have been very, very few – has been richly compensated by the frequent gains. What's more, I have enjoyed every minute of it for, unlike its soporific elder brother, the weak no trump is vibrant, stimulating and brings an excitement to the game which makes winning a real pleasure.'

What can I say?

Here is Rixi Markus, probably the greatest woman player who ever lived, to put the case for the strong 1NT (15-17 points).

'During my long bridge career I have played various systems, but only twice do I remember ever playing a weak no trump. On both occasions, the player I gave into was Nico Gardener. We played a variable no trump – i.e. he opened a weak no trump and I never did!

Here is my case for the strong no trump. In one bid you can tell your partner everything – that you hold 15-17 balanced points and (if you play by my rules) no suit holding is worse than Qx or Jxx. You deduct 1 point for QJ bare and the same for KQ or AK bare because it reduces the value in a no trump contract.

The advantages of using this excellent weapon are as follows:

1. *The opponents rarely venture to interfere and you will often buy the contract cheaply.*

2. *If they do come in your partner can punish their boldness. Here is an example. Playing with Patrick Jourdain in Holland, I held:*

> ♠ *1098x*
> ♡ *xxx*
> ◇ *AK10x*
> ♣ *9x*

Patrick opened 1NT as dealer, my RHO bid 2♠ and I doubled for +800. Had Patrick opened 1♣, 1◊ or 1♡ and RHO overcalled 1♠, I could hardly have doubled.

3. *Instead of bidding a weak no trump I like to bid the suit I want led. If I bid 1NT partner has to work harder to find the best lead when the opponents but the contract.*

4. *I don't like to announce to the whole world that I am weak! With a call in a suit I might hold up to 20 points, and if the other side play the hand they will have to guess how many points I hold.*

5. *Some of my greatest triumphs have been when I was able to punish the weak no trump. Nico Gardener never bid a weak no trump without a possible escape, but most people just count up to 12-14 points irrespective of unprotected queens and jacks.*

6. *Against weak players you do not need a weak no trump, but the strong no trump will pre-empt them and you want you be declarer when you hold AQ, KJ10 or any other tenaces.*

7. *To finish, I would agree that there are certain merits in any sensible system or convention applied with commonsense, but the strong no trump has hardly any disadvantages and is essential if you play Acol or any other rational system where a bid at the one level is limited.*

Therefore there must be a bid to express a balanced holding of 15-17 points. It often is a good resting place, and saves a lot of bidding space. Many good players play the strong no trump, especially in France, one of the strongholds of bridge in Europe.'

From my umpire's chair, I reckon it's a draw. This leads me nicely on to the clinching argument. The theoreticians can slug it out for as long as they like, in reality which method is best boils down to *your* temperament. If you can accept the occasional disaster with equanimity, use a weak 1NT. If not, go for its stronger brother. Only you know the answer to that!

7

DON'T BE NERVOUS, IT WON'T HURT

Although bridge is a partnership game, there is one aspect of play which enables the 'individual' to shine. When the dummy is put down, declarer is on his own. Now all the flair and imagination which you might have to bottle up during the auction can come forth.

Thus to be known as one of the 'great declarers' is an accolade that is highly sought after. In the modern game, my personal choice of the 'greatest' would be Jeff Meckstroth (USA) and here's why ....

The best declarers make defenders nervous and nervous defenders make mistakes. You wouldn't want to meet Meckstroth in a dark alley, but that is not why he terrorises defenders. Tricks just seem to materialise from nowhere as we shall soon see from the next deal. Assess South's chances of making 4♠ for yourself, before reading how Meckstroth tackled the challenge:

Love All. Dealer West.

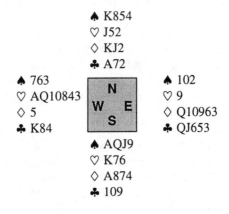

                    ♠ K854
                    ♡ J52
                    ◇ KJ2
                    ♣ A72

    ♠ 763   ♠ 102
    ♡ AQ10843   N   ♡ 9
    ◇ 5   W   E   ◇ Q10963
    ♣ K84   S   ♣ QJ653

                    ♠ AQJ9
                    ♡ K76
                    ◇ A874
                    ♣ 109

West	North	East	South
2♡(i)	Dble(ii)	Pass	4♠
All Pass			

(i)   A weak two bid, 6 to 10 points and a six card suit.
(ii) Takeout – not recommended!

Despite South's excellent hand, dummy has fallen well short of expectation and there seems little hope for the contract. Surely declarer must lose two hearts, one club and one diamond. You would think so, but read on ….

West led ◇ 5, and South played low in dummy, capturing East's ◇ 9 with his ace. Trumps were drawn in three rounds (East pitching ♣3) and declarer casually led a heart towards the jack. West considered for a while and elected to play low, so dummy's ♡J held the trick. A flesh wound for the defence, but hardly fatal.

South now led a low club from dummy, East's ♣J winning. With nothing better to do, East continued with a club to the king and ace. A third round was taken by the ♣Q whilst South discarded ♡7.

Faced with the prospect of leading into ◇ KJ, East pressed on with clubs. Had declarer ruffed in either hand, he would still be a trick short of his contract (five spades, two diamonds, a heart and a club), but he didn't ruff. He threw hearts from both hands!

Now East, who earlier pitched ♣3 remember, *had* to lead a diamond and Meckstroth claimed his tenth winner. Great play.

If you thought that was good, how about this?

East/West Game. Dealer West.

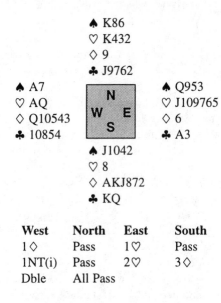

♠ K86
♥ K432
♦ 9
♣ J9762

♠ A7
♥ AQ
♦ Q10543
♣ 10854

♠ Q953
♥ J109765
♦ 6
♣ A3

♠ J1042
♥ 8
♦ AKJ872
♣ KQ

West	North	East	South
1◇	Pass	1♡	Pass
1NT(i)	Pass	2♡	3◇
Dble	All Pass		

(i) Showing 12 to 14 points, East/West were playing a strong 1NT.

Meckstroth's (South) 3◇ would not meet with everyone's approval and surely he was about to get his true desserts. With three aces to lose and at least two trumps to add to that, he was destined for a fall. However ....

West led ♡A and switched, to a club. East took his ace and continued clubs. Meckstroth won and advanced ◇J! West could not believe that his partner did not hold a high diamond, so he played low. Disaster ....

South next tried a spade, West rose with ♠A and returned ♠7. Declarer won ♠K, cashed ♡K and ♣J, pitching two losing spades, and ruffed a club. With four cards left he took ◇A and then led ◇8. West won ◇10, but had to lead away from ◇Q5 at the death.

On the British stage, we have few such scene stealers. One that springs to mind instantly, however, is John Collings. He has been at the top of our tree for almost 30 years now, but has not lost any of his immense card-playing talent. Many years ago, at the rubber bridge table, he made one of the most remarkable hands in history and this is how he did it ....

North/South Game. Dealer South.

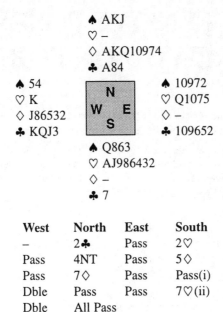

                    ♠ AKJ
                    ♡ –
                    ◊ AKQ10974
                    ♣ A84

    ♠ 54   ♠ 10972
    ♡ K   ♡ Q1075
    ◊ J86532   ◊ –
    ♣ KQJ3   ♣ 109652

                    ♠ Q863
                    ♡ AJ986432
                    ◊ –
                    ♣ 7

West	North	East	South
–	2♣	Pass	2♡
Pass	4NT	Pass	5◊
Pass	7◊	Pass	Pass(i)
Dble	Pass	Pass	7♡(ii)
Dble	All Pass		

(i)   Give North the benefit of the doubt, but ….
(ii) Not any longer.

Faced with the prospect of trying to make 7♡ with a trump suit lacking many vital statistics, Collings (South) set about his task with relish. Impossible? Read on ….

The ♣K was led, South played the ace and casually led ◊A so that he could discard his void club. Quick as a flash, East ruffed with ♡5 and declarer overruffed. A spade to the ace followed, so that ◊K could be led. East was not going to be caught, however, so he ruffed low. Declarer overruffed and entered dummy with ♠K. The ◊Q came next, and almost unbelievably, East ruffed low for the third time. Collings over-ruffed and laid down ♡A, felling both the outstanding honours. 'We were lucky the trumps broke, partner,' said John, gloating somewhat.

Hard though it is to credit, that was a true story. East's name is withheld to protect the criminally potty!

8

DEFENSIVE POSERS, ARE YOU ON FORM?

Posing defensive problems on paper is not quite as simple a task as you might imagine. The difficulty arises because the narrative usually 'ends' at the crucial point. Hence, the solver has the knowledge that it is probably time to do something clever. Unfortunately, at the table, we are not granted such luxuries. Declarer rarely turns to a defender to say 'I'd think a bit longer over this, if I were you!'.

By way of a change, therefore, let us look at a deal, seeing all 52 cards from the beginning and assess the merits of the play.

North/South Game. Dealer East.

```
                    ♠ K74
                    ♡ AK85
                    ◇ 86
                    ♣ A862
      ♠ 96                        ♠ QJ853
      ♡ Q92          N            ♡ J106
      ◇ AQJ9      W     E         ◇ 10742
      ♣ J953          S           ♣ K
                    ♠ A102
                    ♡ 743
                    ◇ K53
                    ♣ Q1074
```

West	North	East	South
–	–	Pass	Pass
1◇(i)	Dble	1♠	2♣(ii)
Pass	Pass	2◇	3♣
All Pass			

(i)   A light opening, designed to get a diamond lead.
(ii) 1NT might have been a better choice.

The bidding simmers gently rather than erupting into activity. East/West, and particularly West for his cheeky 1◇ opening, have done well to push their opponents to the three level. Normally the sequence would have been:

West	North	East	South
–	–	Pass	Pass
Pass	1NT	All Pass	

1NT would have made comfortably on the probable spade lead.

However, North/South were hassled to 3♣, South having to act a second time when East refused to allow him to declare 2♣. Could the defence benefit from their efforts in the auction?

West led ♠9 which went to the jack and ace. Declarer led a club to the ace, noting the fall of East's ♣K, and continued with three rounds of hearts, West taking ♡Q. A second spade was captured in dummy and the thirteenth heart played, South pitching ♠10. West did not want to ruff, because he would be forced into an embarrassing return, as the diagram below shows:

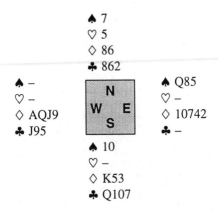

```
                    ♠ 7
                    ♡ 5
                    ◇ 86
                    ♣ 862
   ♠ –                              ♠ Q85
   ♡ –           ┌─────────┐        ♡ –
   ◇ AQJ9        │    N    │        ◇ 10742
   ♣ J95         │  W   E  │        ♣ –
                 │    S    │
                 └─────────┘
                    ♠ 10
                    ♡ –
                    ◇ K53
                    ♣ Q107
```

If West ruffs, he must lead away from one of his minor suit holdings, giving declarer a cheap trick. Instead he threw ◇9, but it was only a temporary reprieve. South ruffed ♠7 in hand, leaving West in an identical predicament. Again, he pitched a diamond, but declarer simply cashed ♣Q and led a club. West could win two trumps, but was forced (eventually) to lead away from ◇AQ. Neatly played by South, but could the defence do better?

As one might suspect, the answer is 'yes'. The culprit is West, but where did he go wrong? He had failed to see the importance of getting East on lead. Then a diamond switch would kill any chance of declarer organising an end-play later. Thus, West should follow with ♡Q to the *second* round of the suit. That would enable East to get in with ♡J and find the key play.

It is much harder to detect this 'unblock' when playing the whole thirteen tricks, than if the play had paused at the crucial moment. Anyone who states that part-scores are dull and that excitement in bridge is confined to the 'big' deals, clearly does not enjoy the intricacies of the game. I will always be fascinated by hands like the one above.

So, the art of being a good defender is to be alert at all times. No one taps us on the shoulder to say 'this is the key moment', and as a result we always need to have our wits about us.

Here are a couple of situations where East has a chance to defeat the contract; see how you get on:

East/West Game. Dealer North.

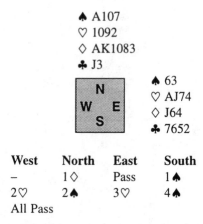

♠ A107
♡ 1092
◇ AK1083
♣ J3

♠ 63
♡ AJ74
◇ J64
♣ 7652

West	North	East	South
–	1◇	Pass	1♠
2♡	2♠	3♡	4♠
All Pass			

Partner leads ♡K against South's 4♠ contract, how do you visualise the defence?

The second hand is:

North/South Game. Dealer South.

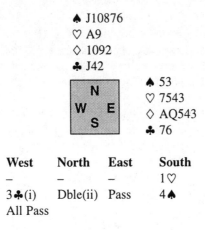

♠ J10876
♡ A9
◇ 1092
♣ J42

♠ 53
♡ 7543
◇ AQ543
♣ 76

West	North	East	South
–	–	–	1♡
3♣(i)	Dble(ii)	Pass	4♠
All Pass			

(i)   A pre-emptive jump overcall.
(ii) Showing 4+ spades and (usually) at least 8 points.

West leads ♣A, ♣K and a small club, how do you proceed?

On our first hand, you have to seize the opportunity to obtain the lead, and trick one is going to be your only chance. Once in, you can fire a club through declarer and partner can take his trick(s) in the suit before they run away.

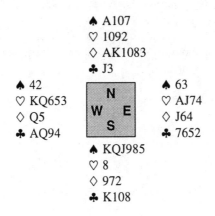

♠ A107
♡ 1092
◇ AK1083
♣ J3

♠ 42
♡ KQ653
◇ Q5
♣ AQ94

♠ 63
♡ AJ74
◇ J64
♣ 7652

♠ KQJ985
♡ 8
◇ 972
♣ K108

At the table, East encouraged with ♡7 and West continued the suit. Declarer still had to play with great skill to land his contract. He ruffed and led a diamond to North's king. Next came two rounds of trumps ending in his hand and a further diamond towards dummy.

When West's queen appeared, declarer ducked(!) the trick. West was stuck on play. He could either cash ♣A then, or allow South to pitch two clubs on the diamonds and take his trick at the end. A neat 'avoidance' play by declarer, assisted by East's lack of awareness at trick one.

On the second hand, West wants you to ruff his club with your *highest* trump in the hope that you will promote a trick in trumps. If you couldn't be bothered playing ♠5, the full layout will make you weep!

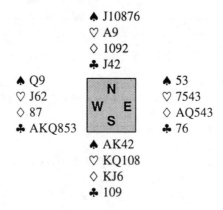

```
                    ♠ J10876
                    ♡ A9
                    ◇ 1092
                    ♣ J42
        ♠ Q9                      ♠ 53
        ♡ J62        N            ♡ 7543
        ◇ 87      W     E         ◇ AQ543
        ♣ AKQ853     S            ♣ 76
                    ♠ AK42
                    ♡ KQ108
                    ◇ KJ6
                    ♣ 109
```

The effect of playing your modest ♠5 is dramatic indeed. Declarer must use one of his top honours to overruff and in the process, West's ♠Q becomes a trick. If you casually throw on ♠3, declarer can win with ♠4, cash ♠AK and go about his business. In such situations, it is best to try and hide ♠5 from sight!

Are you in the mood now? OK.

Quiz

It's time for you to get that thinking cap on as I present 'Six of the Best'.
Good luck, and beware of tricks!

1. Love All. Dealer South.

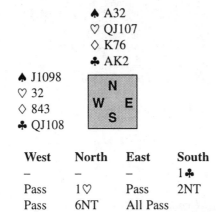

```
              ♠ A32
              ♡ QJ107
              ◊ K76
              ♣ AK2
♠ J1098     ┌─────────┐
♡ 32        │    N    │
◊ 843       │ W     E │
♣ QJ108     │    S    │
            └─────────┘
```

West	North	East	South
–	–	–	1♣
Pass	1♡	Pass	2NT
Pass	6NT	All Pass	

You lead ♠J, which is won by declarer's king and, at trick two, South
plays ♣5. How do you propose to defeat the contract?

2. Game All. Dealer South.

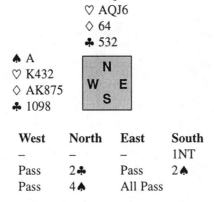

```
              ♠ KQJ7
              ♡ AQJ6
              ◊ 64
              ♣ 532
♠ A         ┌─────────┐
♡ K432      │    N    │
◊ AK875     │ W     E │
♣ 1098      │    S    │
            └─────────┘
```

West	North	East	South
–	–	–	1NT
Pass	2♣	Pass	2♠
Pass	4♠	All Pass	

You lead ◊A which goes 4, 2, 9. How do you proceed?

3. Love All. Dealer East.

♠ K106
♡ J8642
◇ K7
♣ 1084

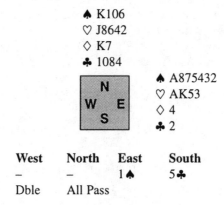

♠ A875432
♡ AK53
◇ 4
♣ 2

West	North	East	South
–	–	1♠	5♣
Dble	All Pass		

West leads ♠Q, declarer playing low in dummy. What is your plan of campaign?

4. East/West Game. Dealer North.

♠ Q652
♡ J104
◇ A953
♣ K6

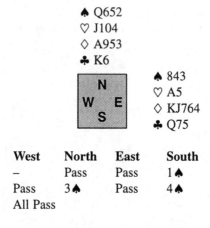

♠ 843
♡ A5
◇ KJ764
♣ Q75

West	North	East	South
–	Pass	Pass	1♠
Pass	3♠	Pass	4♠
All Pass			

West leads ♡3 to your ace and your heart return is taken by South's king. A club to ♣K is followed by a low diamond. How do you defend from here?

5. East/West Game. Dealer North.

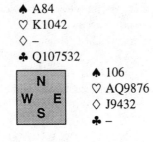

```
              ♠ A84
              ♡ K1042
              ◇ –
              ♣ Q107532
                              ♠ 106
                              ♡ AQ9876
                              ◇ J9432
                              ♣ –
```

West	North	East	South
–	Pass	Pass	1♠
Pass	2♣	2♡	3♠
Pass	4♠	All Pass	

West leads ♡5 to your queen, declarer following with ♡3. What now?

6. East/West Game. Dealer West.

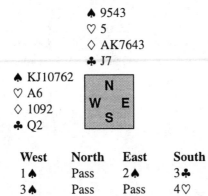

```
                        ♠ 9543
                        ♡ 5
                        ◇ AK7643
                        ♣ J7
      ♠ KJ10762
      ♡ A6
      ◇ 1092
      ♣ Q2
```

West	North	East	South
1♠	Pass	2♠	3♣
3♠	Pass	Pass	4♡
Pass	5♣	All Pass	

Your rather dubious 3♠ bid has helped your opponents into game. Can you justify your actions by rising to the challenge? You lead ◇10, won in dummy with the king whilst East plays ◇5. Declarer leads a heart and after a short pause, plays ♡9. You win ♡A and …?

Solutions

1. This problem is very hard to see as a defender, so anyone who found
    the answer can be pleased with themselves. Given our club holding, it
    seems strange that declarer should begin by tackling the suit.

In fact, South is about to duck a trick in the suit to improve his chances of
success. Let me show you the full deal to help explain the process:

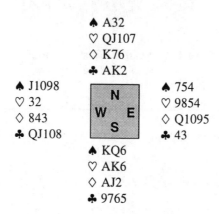

```
                    ♠ A32
                    ♡ QJ107
                    ◊ K76
                    ♣ AK2
  ♠ J1098                        ♠ 754
  ♡ 32         N                 ♡ 9854
  ◊ 843      W   E               ◊ Q1095
  ♣ QJ108        S               ♣ 43
                    ♠ KQ6
                    ♡ AK6
                    ◊ AJ2
                    ♣ 9765
```

After a club has been ducked, South will win the return and lead out
♣AK, testing to see if the suit divides evenly. When East shows out, he
will resort to the winning diamond finesse and make his contract.

We have a Mission Impossible. We must stop declarer in his tracks, and
there is a way. If we follow with ♣10, South might believe that the suit is
distributed thus:

```
              AK2

      J10              Q843

              9765
```

Now he can win the king of clubs and try the ace. Again, we must be
vigilant and play ♣J (or the queen) continuing to fool South. Surely he
will play a third club expecting to establish his ♣9, rather than risk a
50/50 proposition in diamonds?

2. A quick count of the points will tell you that we are on our own here.
    Partner will have at most one jack. Thus, there is no prospect of
    striking gold with a club switch and a heart seems pointless. All we
    are left with is continuing diamonds and trust to luck:

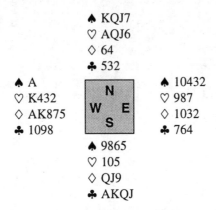

```
                    ♠ KQJ7
                    ♡ AQJ6
                    ◇ 64
                    ♣ 532
     ♠ A                          ♠ 10432
     ♡ K432          N            ♡ 987
     ◇ AK875      W     E         ◇ 1032
     ♣ 1098          S            ♣ 764
                    ♠ 9865
                    ♡ 105
                    ◇ QJ9
                    ♣ AKQJ
```

We play the ace and king of diamonds and a third round, taken by South.
After winning ♠A, a fourth round of diamonds will promote ♠10 in
East's hand. Despite holding the most miserable of collections, partner
will take the setting trick.

3.

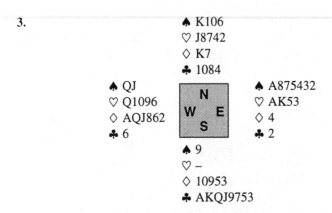

```
                    ♠ K106
                    ♡ J8742
                    ◇ K7
                    ♣ 1084
     ♠ QJ                         ♠ A875432
     ♡ Q1096          N           ♡ AK53
     ◇ AQJ862      W     E        ◇ 4
     ♣ 6             S            ♣ 2
                    ♠ 9
                    ♡ –
                    ◇ 10953
                    ♣ AKQJ9753
```

Only one defence is certain to beat 5♣ doubled, and it is not easy to see.
East has to overtake ♠Q with the ace and return a diamond to West's ◇A.
A second round of diamonds secures a ruff.

Whilst it is possible that West might switch to ◊ A if ♠Q holds the trick, it is extremely unlikely. In practice he will probably stroke his chin, gaze at the ceiling and then continue with ♠J.

4.

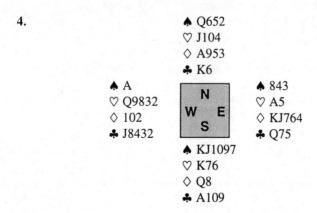

      ♠ Q652
      ♡ J104
      ◊ A953
      ♣ K6

♠ A   ♠ 843
♡ Q9832   ♡ A5
◊ 102   ◊ KJ764
♣ J8432   ♣ Q75

      ♠ KJ1097
      ♡ K76
      ◊ Q8
      ♣ A109

To put ourselves in the frame, we must rise with ◊ K. Not too tough that part, the problem is what next? It looks tempting to play a diamond back or even a club.

Declarer would win the return, cash the other minor suit winner and ruff a club. Then he would lead ◊ A, pitching his losing heart. Of course, West would ruff, but with ♠A! South would be home.

The only path to glory is for East to play a trump after collecting ◊ K. West can win ♠A and cash ♡Q to defeat the contract. I said beware of tricks!

5.

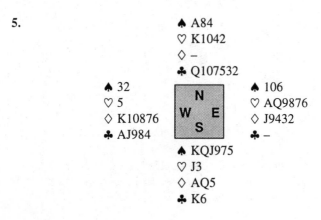

      ♠ A84
      ♡ K1042
      ◊ –
      ♣ Q107532

♠ 32   ♠ 106
♡ 5   ♡ AQ9876
◊ K10876   ◊ J9432
♣ AJ984   ♣ –

      ♠ KQJ975
      ♡ J3
      ◊ AQ5
      ♣ K6

It sure looks tempting to lay down ♡A and follow with another heart. What will happen? Declarer ruffs with ♠J and draw trumps in two rounds, before leading ♣K. With the marked club finesse available and ♡K still in dummy, there are ample parking places for diamond losers.

However, East can foil declarer by rejecting the obvious course of action. If he returns ♡6, rather than cash ♡A first, he will force West to ruff. Hopefully partner can then work out that a club continuation is required, and consequently declarer will lose the first four tricks.

6.
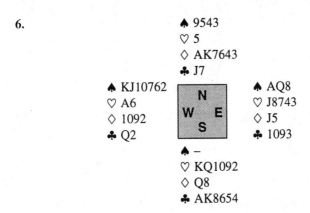

```
                    ♠ 9543
                    ♡ 5
                    ◇ AK7643
                    ♣ J7
  ♠ KJ10762                      ♠ AQ8
  ♡ A6            N              ♡ J8743
  ◇ 1092      W       E          ◇ J5
  ♣ Q2            S              ♣ 1093
                    ♠ –
                    ♡ KQ1092
                    ◇ Q8
                    ♣ AK8654
```

We must not allow declarer the privilege of ruffing hearts in dummy. However, if we switch to a low club, South will be home. He rises with ♣J in dummy and ruffs a spade. Then he trumps a heart and returns to ◇Q to draw the defence's clubs. That line of play provides a comfortable eleven tricks. No good at all.

The answer is to switch to ♣Q! Although this sets up ♣J, South cannot ruff a heart without setting up a winner for East. One way or another, the defence must come to three tricks.

Congratulations to those who correctly solved three or more of these teasers. You now have 'A' level bridge, watch out for the 'degree' course! If you were successful on *all* those problems, and you do not have a partner at present, when are you free for a game?

9

WHEN TO TEACH THE OPPONENTS A LESSON

'Never double for one down,' my father used to say. Sadly, this helpful advice was often given just after we allowed declarer to steal a trick and make his contract. I always agreed at the time, of course, but in my heart nothing had changed. I still love to double the opponents.

There are three arguments against tight doubles:

1. The declarer may be able to take an extra trick by placing the cards accurately.
2. The defence feels under pressure and is more inclined to wilt and concede an extra trick.

I said 'three', and I will illustrate the third by way of this bidding problem.

You are East and hold the following hand:

♠ A42
♡ K1097
♢ A54
♣ K107

The bidding to date has been:

West	North	East	South
Pass	1♡	Pass	1♠
Pass	3♡	Pass	3NT
Pass	4♡	?	

North deliberates a long time over his partner's 3NT and eventually removes to 4♡. With two certain trump tricks and two aces, it looks time to wield the axe. 'Double' you say, confident that this *is* the occasion when you can safely double for one down.

The bidding now takes a strange turn:

West	North	East	South
Pass	1♡	Pass	1♠
Pass	3♡	Pass	3NT
Pass	4♡	Dble	Pass
Pass	4♠	?	

'In for a penny ....' You decide to double again, although on less firm ground this time. Maybe you have them on the run, but that little man in the pit of your stomach doesn't think so. The bidding concludes and your partner makes the most sensible lead of a trump.

East/West Game. Dealer West.

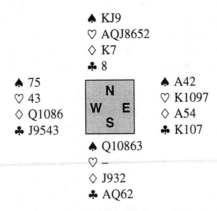

```
              ♠ KJ9
              ♡ AQJ8652
              ◇ K7
              ♣ 8
   ♠ 75                      ♠ A42
   ♡ 43           N          ♡ K1097
   ◇ Q1086    W     E        ◇ A54
   ♣ J9543         S         ♣ K107
              ♠ Q10863
              ♡ –
              ◇ J932
              ♣ AQ62
```

You win the first trick with ♠A and return a second round of spades, still feeling reasonably confident. However, the first 'downside' of your initial double comes to the fore, because South can picture the entire hand and thus play 'double dummy'.

The trump return is won in dummy, and ♡A taken on which declarer pitches a club. He continues with ♡Q, you cover and South ruffs.

The ♣A and a club ruff follow. Declarer then cashes ♡J, throwing a diamond, and ruffs another heart.

So far, the defence have one trick and this is the position with five cards remaining:

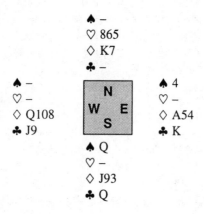

The last trump is drawn and now the *coup de grâce* is applied. South advances ♣Q, putting you on lead. With only diamonds remaining you have no alternative but to cash ◇A and concede the balance to dummy.

A very well-played hand by declarer, but only made possible by your initial double of 4♡, and your subsequent double of 4♠ (which suggested that you had more than simply a heart 'stack').

So the third and final reason not to make marginal doubles is that occasionally the opponents can fly the coop and come to rest in a safer haven. It is dangerous to be too quick on the trigger because it is easy to shoot yourself in the foot! I should know, I have limped away from many a session.

Conversely, those of us who are too nervous of doubling can be stolen from. Take this deal for example:

East/West Game. Dealer East.

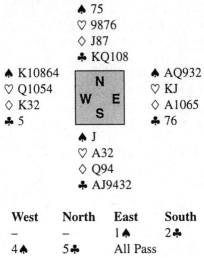

```
                    ♠ 75
                    ♡ 9876
                    ◇ J87
                    ♣ KQ108
  ♠ K10864                        ♠ AQ932
  ♡ Q1054          N              ♡ KJ
  ◇ K32        W       E          ◇ A1065
  ♣ 5              S              ♣ 76
                    ♠ J
                    ♡ A32
                    ◇ Q94
                    ♣ AJ9432
```

West	North	East	South
–	–	1♠	2♣
4♠	5♣	All Pass	

The final contract was not well played. After the spade lead, Declarer won East's switch to ♡K, drew trumps and led ◇Q. West took ◇K, cashed two hearts, and returned a diamond two more tricks. Four down!

Despite his poor effort in the play, South was happy. The opponents had an easy vulnerable game and yet he had to pay just 200 points in compensation. A very good deal indeed. So, who should have doubled 5♣? Let's hear what the players said when the hand was over:

West: 'You heard me bid 4♠, so it was up to you now. Anyway, I only held eight points.'

East: 'I had two tricks at most, and your 4♠ was a barrage bid. You might have had ♠KJxxxx and nothing else.'

Both arguments seem quite plausible at face value, where do *your* sympathies lie? Who do you think shoulders the lion's share of the blame?

For me, both players were guilty of excessive caution. The point at issue is not whether they could have had more strength, but whether they could have had less. Neither hand was minimum, particularly in terms of defensive strength.

Two other points are worth mentioning:

1.   At such a high level there is no need to have good trumps in order to double, sheer weight of numbers will defeat most contracts.

2.   Do not expect to defeat the contract on your own. When your side has bid to game, with an expectation of success, your combined forces will be what counts. Put another way, you can afford to assume that partner has some useful bits and pieces.

We really should have heard that rare post-mortem:

West: 'Sorry, partner.'
East: 'Sorry, partner!'

So, how *do* we assess the correct time to double, and when to keep our own counsel? I addressed this point in 1994 ....

One of the qualities for an expert player to possess is knowing when to double. Here are a couple of examples to illustrate how to develop one's thinking during the sequence, and to put the conclusions into action.

North/South Game. Dealer South.

♠ KJ87
♡ 8642
◇ KJ92
♣ 6

West	North	East	South
–	–	–	1◇
Pass	1♡	Pass	1♠
Pass	1NT	Pass	2NT
Pass	3NT	Pass	Pass
?			

Let us delve into the mind of an expert West. He is first pleased to hear South open 1◇ because he can visualise the instant improvement in his hand. Suddenly ◇KJ92 feels more like ◇KQJ2. Better news is to come, as South continues with spades at his next turn.

West should formulate the view that he wants North/South to push as high as possible, because all the finesses will be wrong.

The whole picture is not complete yet, however, for West is unsure to date, of the total strength of his opponent's cards. This becomes evident when North limits his hand by responding 1NT and South invites game by raising.

When North accepts the invitation, and 3NT is passed round to West, the expert will ponder these facts:

1.   North/South have minimum values for game.

2.   All the key suits lie badly.

3.   Partner's likely to make a disastrous lead lead without guidance (holding length in the unbid suit).

All the above tempts our expert into doubling the final contract, visualising a layout such as:

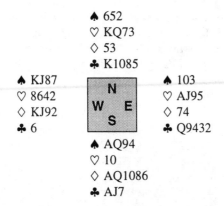

```
                    ♠ 652
                    ♡ KQ73
                    ◇ 53
                    ♣ K1085
        ♠ KJ87                      ♠ 103
        ♡ 8642          N           ♡ AJ95
        ◇ KJ92      W       E       ◇ 74
        ♣ 6             S           ♣ Q9432
                    ♠ AQ94
                    ♡ 10
                    ◇ AQ1086
                    ♣ AJ7
```

The potential penalty on a spade lead (assuming partner is alive to the situation), is considerable, and can create points out of nothing. As a corollary, note how the position alters if you had been East. Now it's all doom and gloom.

Listening to the bidding is a key aspect and, again, is evident in our second example, a play problem sent in by Mr. Bennett of Dumfries.

North/South Game. Dealer South.

♠ K743
♡ 64
◇ KQ10942
♣ 9

♠ A65
♡ AK10875
◇ 7
♣ QJ4

West	North	East	South
–	–	–	1♡
Pass	2◇	Pass	3♡
Pass	4♡	Dble	All Pass

West began with ◇A and switched to ♠J. Declarer won in hand and exited a low club, taken by West's 10. The ♠10 was continued and East dropped ♠Q under dummy's King. Now ◇K was cashed, South discarded a spade and ◇Q was ruffed by East with ♡Q and overruffed.

A club ruff in dummy left this position.

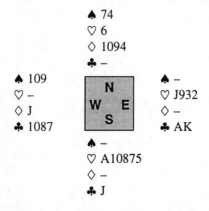

♠ 74
♡ 6
◇ 1094
♣ –

♠ 109
♡ –
◇ J
♣ 1087

♠ –
♡ J932
◇ –
♣ AK

♠ –
♡ A10875
◇ –
♣ J

A diamond was ruffed in hand and the last club ruffed in dummy. A spade followed and East was caught. He actually tried the ♡2, but declarer could overruff and exit a small trump.

East won with the nine, but was forced to lead into declarer's ♡A10 for the last two tricks.

Not only was it a disaster to allow this hand to make, but additionally catastrophic was the fact that it would never have been made without the double. Declarer could place all the opposing cards and this enabled him to succeed.

The major difference between the last two doubles was that one simply announced that the cards were badly placed for declarer, so could not lose anything, whereas the other gave away valuable and helpful information. It cost him dear.

10
WHAT IS A MULLIGAN?

A couple of years ago I played my first round of golf in the United States. Having seen many wonderful courses on television, I was naturally very excited at the prospect, and as I arrived at the first tee and surveyed more water than grass, I was not disappointed.

'We play Mulligans' my American host informed me, but I had absolutely no idea what he was talking about.

'OK.' I said, trying to hide my ignorance of what it meant.

He teed off first and sent his opening drive for a swim, disturbing a couple of not-too-startled ducks into the bargain. I moved forward to have my go, at which point, he put down another ball and drove it down the fairway.

'That's my Mulligan', he said, picking up his tee-peg triumphantly.

How wonderful it would be to use an occasional Mulligan at bridge. Les Steel, the Scottish and British International, would no doubt have appreciated one on this hand:

East/West Game. Dealer East.

♠ 6
♡ A107
♢ KJ6
♣ Q109432

♠ AQ8742
♡ J654
♢ –
♣ AJ7

West	North	East	South
–	–	Pass	1♠
Pass	1NT(1)	2♢	2♡
3♢	3♡	Pass	Pass
4♢	Pass	Pass	4♡
Dble	All Pass		

(i)   Up to 11 points

The bidding warrants a little explanation and commentary. North's response of 1NT to South's opening 1♠ appears somewhat strange, but the partnership were playing a method whereby a two-level reply guaranteed at least 11 points.

After North's 3♡ bid, South was tempted to go straight to game, but decided to make a tactical pass, hoping to be pushed into 4♡. Sure enough, West came back to life and South's coup appeared complete when he was doubled.

However, dummy's 3-card support and wasted diamond strength was hugely disappointing, and despair was the order of the day. Steel ruffed the lead of ♢ A, and played a heart to West's queen, which he ducked in dummy.

Another diamond to the jack and queen was ruffed by declarer, who now led a heart to the ten. Sadly, East showed out. Eventually, declarer sank to a two-trick defeat, no doubt wishing that his partner had doubled 4♢. This was the full deal:

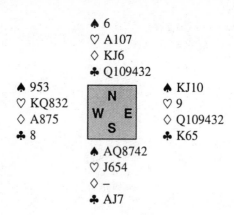

Now, let us replace our emotional Scotsman, with a cold-hearted computer named 'Mulligan'. He is completely unruffled at the sight of an uninspiring dummy, and just goes about his business as usual. He ruffs ◇A and plays a heart as before, but instead of ducking, he wins ♡A over West's queen.

A spade to the queen, is followed by ♠A and a spade, ruffed in dummy. After a club to the jack comes another spade. We have reached:

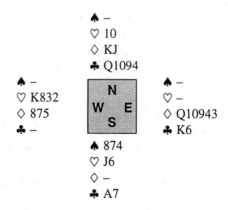

To discard will do West's cause no good, as declarer has several winning spades to play, so let us assume that he ruffs with ♡2 (it doesn't help to ruff with ♡K, I can assure you). Dummy over-ruffs and continues with ♣Q, and again West must use a trump: down to ♡K8.

A diamond is led, but North rises with ◇ K and continues clubs. Although West collects three trump tricks, he cannot find another winner to go with them. The contract is duly made.

As we don't have Mulligans at the table, remember to fight that despair at trick one and give every contract your best attention *first time round!*

In fact, care at trick one is vital for declarer and defence alike. Not that I can preach on this matter.

As a bridge player, I have been plagued with two failings that I would be delighted to correct. First, I tend to 'sacrifice' at the drop of a hat, and secondly I often play too quickly, particularly at the first trick.

Let me give you an example of the latter in action. Take declarer's chair for a moment:

East/West Game. Dealer South.

♠ K92
♡ 654
◇ A
♣ A109652

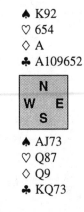

♠ AJ73
♡ Q87
◇ Q9
♣ KQ73

West	North	East	South
–	–	–	1♣(i)
3◇	4◇(ii)	Pass	5♣
All Pass			

(i)   Playing a strong no trump and five card majors
(ii) Cuebid, showing a slam try in clubs

West leads ♠10 against your 5♣ contract. What a good start! Isn't it a reflex reaction to call for a small card from dummy and win in hand with ♠J? It would, however, be a fatal error as a look at the spade suit in isolation will show us:

After ♠10 has run to the jack, declarer will later play ♠K and follow with the nine. However, East will be able to cover with ♠Q leaving South with ♠7 and East ♠8. In all, three tricks have been won by South.

To achieve the vital fourth trick, it is necessary to rise with ♠K at trick one. Then when next in dummy, lead the nine, forcing East to cover. Return to North and finesse ♠A7 which is now 'over' East's ♠86.

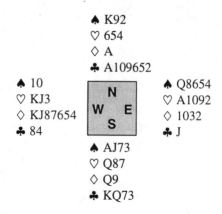

Once the optimum play in spades is deduced, the contract is easy. Declarer wins ♠K, draws the trumps ending in dummy and leads ♠9. Even if East covers, it is simple to return to dummy via ◊A to play spades again. Eventually a losing heart can be discarded and two hearts conceded. West could, of course, have beaten the hand by leading hearts, but no one could blame him for his actual choice.

Here is another example of haste causing waste, or how not to fall at the first hurdle:

North/South Game. Dealer South.

♠ K94
♡ 872
◇ 7654
♣ A65

♠ A8765
♡ A6
◇ AK
♣ K432

West	North	East	South
–	–	–	1♠
Pass	1NT(i)	Pass	3♣(ii)
Pass	4♠(iii)	All Pass	

(i)   A raise to 2♠ is preferable, but that's another story
(ii)   Forcing to game
(iii) Showing genuine support for spades

Rather surprisingly given the bidding, West leads ♣J. South drew the conclusion that this must be a singleton, otherwise why lead declarer's second suit?

He won in hand with ♣K and drew two rounds of trumps. Now he continued with ♣A. East following with the queen and another club on which East showed out. Sadly for South, West won the club and continued with ♠Q, drawing dummy's last trump. He could cash his remaining club and wait for a heart in the wash. South lost two clubs, one spade and a heart.

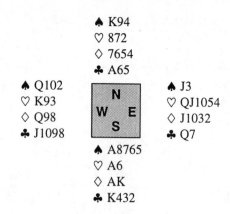

The line of play adopted was reasonable and was slightly unlucky to fail. However, the contract was fool-proof if spades divided 3-2.

Declarer was too concerned about the motives behind the opening lead, and this allowed his mind to wander from the job in hand. As you will have gathered, his error was at trick one. Consider the developments if South ducks ♣J in both hands.

Should West continue clubs, declarer wins the trick with ♣A and draws two rounds of trumps. It does not matter who has ♠Q, or when they choose to use it, South cannot be prevented from ruffing a club in dummy. Declarer must ensure that the defence cannot play a third round of trumps, after he has drawn the first two.

Winning the club lead gave West a late entry, and when he held the last trump, the contract was defeated. That was an unnecessary risk. Careful thought at trick one would have saved the day. So remember the next time dummy goes down ... think!

11
SHOULD YOU USE
HAND SIGNALS?

One of the characteristics which makes bridge different from nearly all other card games is the co-operation between partners. To be more exact, the way that players 'signal' what they hold when defending, and which suit they would like led.

I thought it might be interesting to look at some of the common situations which occur, and see how accurate signalling can come to our aid. Incidentally, do not fall foul of the 'I never signal, it gives too much away' brigade. They are solo players, in more ways than one!

No, the signal is one of our few helpers in the struggle to find a sound defence. Look at this classic position:

Love All. Dealer North.

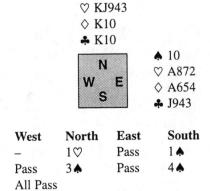

```
                    ♠ AK62
                    ♡ KJ943
                    ◊ K10
                    ♣ K10
                                    ♠ 10
                    N               ♡ A872
              W           E         ◊ A654
                    S               ♣ J943
```

West	North	East	South
–	1♡	Pass	1♠
Pass	3♠	Pass	4♠
All Pass			

West leads ♡10 to our ace, declarer following with ♡Q. How do we propose to defeat the contract?

First, we must not be fooled by South's deception at trick one. Partner is leading dummy's suit with good cause and the most likely reason is that he holds a singleton. So we should return a heart at trick two to give West a ruff. However, to defeat 4♠ we need to regain the lead immediately and repeat the process. For that we must tell West to return a diamond at trick three. This is where our signal comes in.

To announce an entry in the higher-ranking suit (remember West only has diamonds and clubs to choose from), we play back our highest heart (in this case, ♡8).

Finally, if East held ♣A, and not ◇A, he should return ♡2 at trick two (low card for a low-ranking suit). This type of signal is often referred to as '*suit preference*'.

Another important facet of defence is to describe our *distribution*. Armed with that knowledge, partner can make apparently sensational plays, such as the following:

North/South Game. Dealer South.

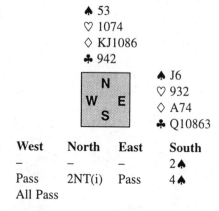

```
            ♠ 53
            ♡ 1074
            ◇ KJ1086
            ♣ 942
                      ♠ J6
         N            ♡ 932
     W       E        ◇ A74
         S            ♣ Q10863
```

West	North	East	South
–	–	–	2♠
Pass	2NT(i)	Pass	4♠
All Pass			

(i)   A negative showing less than one and a half 'quick' tricks, usually defined as an ace and a king

South reaches 4♠ without giving much information away about his hand. In such circumstances, the signal can be crucial in determining the best defensive strategy.

Sitting East, you see partner's lead of ♡Q swallowed up by declarer's king. At trick two, South advances ◊Q and overtakes it with the king. Do you take the ace or not?

To answer that question properly, you need a piece of information which I have deliberately withheld (shame on me!). Which diamond did West play on the second trick? If it was ◊2, then he should signify an odd number of diamonds, if ◊5 or ◊9 he has an even number (High for even, Low for Odd, or HELO).

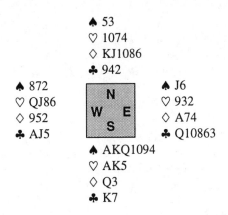

```
            ♠ 53
            ♡ 1074
            ◊ KJ1086
            ♣ 942
♠ 872                     ♠ J6
♡ QJ86         N          ♡ 932
◊ 952        W   E        ◊ A74
♣ AJ5          S          ♣ Q10863
            ♠ AKQ1094
            ♡ AK5
            ◊ Q3
            ♣ K7
```

West should play ◊2 on the second trick. East, knowing from his partner's play that declarer has sneakily hidden his other diamond, ducks ◊K. In this way, he can neutralise dummy's suit and eventually defeat the contract. Without this assistance, the defence would simply have to guess.

So what is the most effective signalling method? Opinions vary as to whether one should provide information about length in a suit, or one's desire to have it played. Put briefly, if one uses 'distributional' or 'attitude' signals. Here are two British greats, sadly no longer with us, putting forward their point of view.

First, Joe Amsbury, in favour of giving the 'count':

"The reason why I am so keen on distributional signals is that any good player can work out what high cards partner needs to beat a contract but, especially in the early tricks, you need second sight to know how many cards declarer holds in a suit. With my

"Give me a count" style, the whole hand is frequently counted after about three tricks – and that means, usually, before I have had time to make a disastrous decision.

I stick to the old-fashioned high-low for an even number, low-high for an odd number, although there does appear to be merit in playing "reverse" signals. Either way, you inevitably give information to declarer as well as to partner, but so must any method of signalling.

With four or more cards you may have a choice. Suppose a low card is led and dummy wins with Ax. Against a no trump contract I would play the nine from either K98x or from 98xx. Against a suit contract I would normally play the nine from K98x, the three from 9832.

The sort of situation where you are especially glad to be playing distributional signals occurs when you lead high from AK10xx against a no trump contract, dummy goes down with xxx, and partner plays the two. Now you can continue high knowing that declarer's queen. If he has it, will fall.

Once a defender has shown how many cards he has in a suit, he can thereafter choose any of the remaining cards to give a suit-preference signal.

Sometimes we can get the best of both worlds. Say partner leads a middle card against a suit contract and dummy wins with the ace. With five small cards you play the lowest, but with K9862 you may consider the eight. Then, if you get a chance to discard the nine, you will have given a clear picture.

To those who say that this gives away too much information, I quote Forquet's reply when the same was said of Italian bidding: "I don't care if the opponent's know every card in my hand. If we are in a solid slam, they can do nothing about it anyway."
Also wrong is the belief that this style of signalling is a strait jacket – in fact, it is relaxed and free-wheeling. Our style can be abandoned at the drop of a hat. As soon as we have a count of the hand, we no longer give accurate information. And on the many

occasions when a count is obviously superfluous, we simply don't
bother to give one.

Hands can always be produced to make a point, but situations like
this are constantly turning up:

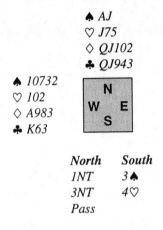

```
               ♠ AJ
               ♡ J75
               ◇ QJ102
               ♣ QJ943
♠ 10732    ┌─────────┐
♡ 102      │    N    │
◇ A983     │  W   E  │
♣ K63      │    S    │
           └─────────┘
```

North	South
1NT	3♠
3NT	4♡
Pass	

As West you lead the ace of diamonds and partner contributes the
seven. What now?

On bidding, South can have at most three minor cards. Partner
has told you that South has only one diamond, so a club switch is
urgent. You switch, therefore, and on a good day make a killing
when you find partner with the ace. Even if declarer has ♣A you
won't have lost anything. Distributional signals make this kind of
defence easy to find.

For the "attitude" camp I present Jeremy Flint:

"It all depends on what you mean by attitude," Professor Joad
would have squeaked. In order to argue the case cogently, the
points of difference must be clearly defined. Everyone signals
distribution to help partners gauge when to release control of
dummy's long suit. Equally, provided the signals will prove of
greater assistance to partner than to the opposition, it is universal
practice to show an odd or even number in a suit. More debatable
is the play to the first trick against a no trump contract. But again,

most modern players accept that it is correct to show the count religiously.

The dichotomy appears when a signal may be construed as encouraging or discouraging by one school and merely as an indication of length by another.

The suit presents a slippery banana skin for the distribution merchants.

♠ 654

♠ KQ10   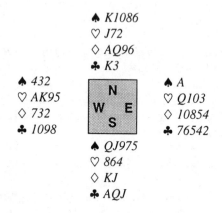   ♠ 9872

♠ AJ3

If the lead of the king proclaims specifically the king-queen, any card from East except the two is prone to produce accidents.

This is another everyday dilemma for distribution signallers.

♠ K1086
♡ J72
◇ AQ96
♣ K3

♠ 432   ♠ A
♡ AK95   ♡ Q103
◇ 732   ◇ 10854
♣ 1098   ♣ 76542

♠ QJ975
♡ 864
◇ KJ
♣ AQJ

The contract is 4♠ by South, after a sequence of 1♠ – 4♠.

West leads the ♡A on which East sagely contributes the ♡3. Nervous that he will lose a vital tempo, West unwisely switches to a minor. Don't tell me he shouldn't, I've seen it happen all too often. Even if West cashes the king of hearts the fish is not in the net, because from 1083 East is expected to play the three and then the ten.

West has nothing to lose by continuing with a third heart? Really? Let us change the setting.

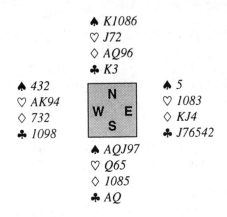

♠ K1086
♡ J72
◇ AQ96
♣ K3

♠ 432
♡ AK94
◇ 732
♣ 1098

♠ 5
♡ 1083
◇ KJ4
♣ J76542

♠ AQJ97
♡ Q65
◇ 1085
♣ AQ

As before, West leads the ♡A. Seeing his partner's discouraging ♡3, an attitude defender would switch. Lacking second sight he might select a club. His partner's ♣2 will tell him that that is not the jar with humbugs in it. When he regains the lead with ♡K, he will push through a diamond to break up the impending end play.

The lesson that emerges from this pair of hands is that attitude signals make it childishly simple for West to find the right defence on both hands. Distributional signals would have given him no assistance whatsoever."

In my view they are both seeing only half the picture. There are just too many situations for one approach to handle, hence, a casserole of the two is preferred by most experts. But, you may be saying, how do you know when to signal what?!

My recipe is the following. Show 'attitude' i.e. a *high* card encourages partner to continue a suit, when *your* side have the lead (HELD), and 'count' (high card shows an even number) when *declarer* is in charge.

To see the importance of attitude signals, try your hand at defending 3♡ on the deal below:

Love All. Dealer West.

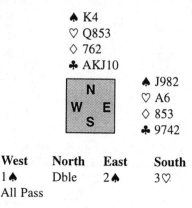

        ♠ K4
        ♡ Q853
        ◊ 762
        ♣ AKJ10

                    ♠ J982
                    ♡ A6
                    ◊ 853
                    ♣ 9742

West	North	East	South
1♠	Dble	2♠	3♡
All Pass			

West leads ♠A, declarer plays low from dummy and it is your turn. Of course, it is easy to say that you cannot possibly desire a second spade from West with the king staring you in the face, but think through the argument more deeply. If you discourage spades, i.e. play ♠2, won't your partner shift to a diamond, the obvious switch? That is not what we want at all.

Strange as it may seem, we need to encourage spades with ♠9 to prevent or discourage a switch to diamonds. In effect, we signal our attitude towards one suit by our action in another.

Our use of cards must be multi-dimensional to cope with the variety of situations that can occur. Flexibility and the ability to think ahead are crucial to successful defending.

To complete this chapter, I have set you a couple of problems on the themes shown above.

Quiz

1. Game All. Dealer East.

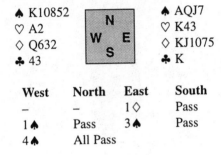

♠ K10852   ♠ AQJ7
♡ A2   ♡ K43
◇ Q632   ◇ KJ1075
♣ 43   ♣ K

West	North	East	South
–	–	1◇	Pass
1♠	Pass	3♠	Pass
4♠	All Pass		

You are West, declaring 4♠ on the lead of ◇9 to South's ace – how do you propose to scramble the enemy signals?

2. Love All. Dealer East.

♠ 6
♡ KJ4
◇ AQ1093
♣ A765

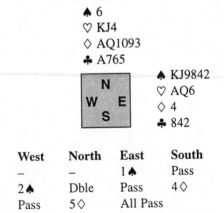

♠ KJ9842
♡ AQ6
◇ 4
♣ 842

West	North	East	South
–	–	1♠	Pass
2♠	Dble	Pass	4◇
Pass	5◇	All Pass	

West leads ♠A against South's 5◇ contract. What do you play at trick one?

Answers

1. Game All. Dealer East.

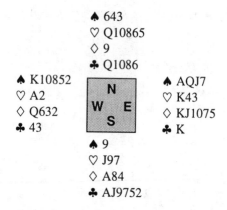

♠ 643
♥ Q10865
♦ 9
♣ Q1086

♠ K10852
♥ A2
♦ Q632
♣ 43

♠ AQJ7
♥ K43
♦ KJ1075
♣ K

♠ 9
♥ J97
♦ A84
♣ AJ9752

It is clear that the threat to 4♠ is from a couple of diamond ruffs. There is little we can do to prevent the first one happening (although we might as well try ◊Q at trick one, just in case). But what can we do about the second?

We must make North think that South is asking for a *heart* return at trick three. If we carefully follow with ◊6 at trick two, North might conclude that ◊4 (which is actually South's lower diamond asking for a club return), is in fact his highest remaining, i.e. he started with ◊A432. At the worst, we have left North with a guess, and a 50% chance is better than none.

2. Love All. Dealer East.

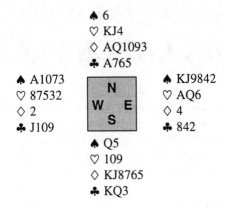

```
                    ♠ 6
                    ♡ KJ4
                    ◇ AQ1093
                    ♣ A765
   ♠ A1073        ┌─────────┐      ♠ KJ9842
   ♡ 87532        │    N    │      ♡ AQ6
   ◇ 2            │ W     E │      ◇ 4
   ♣ J109         │    S    │      ♣ 842
                  └─────────┘
                    ♠ Q5
                    ♡ 109
                    ◇ KJ8765
                    ♣ KQ3
```

The likely continuation from West will be a club, the apparently safer option. Disaster. Declarer is able to pitch a losing heart on the thirteenth club and make his contract. To avert that, throw ♠K under the ace. West should read this as desire to switch to hearts (the higher ranking suit). You would not waste ♠K to encourage spades, a middle card like ♠9 would do that job perfectly adequately. Thus, an unnecessary high card should alert West to what is going on.

If it fails to do so, at least you tried!

12
SHARPEN UP YOUR DECLARER PLAY

I am often asked why experts appear to manage the cards differently to the social player. My answer is to draw on a golfing parallel. An expert is a golfer who carries with him a full set of clubs, and knows exactly which one to use at a given moment. Others, depending on their ability, have fewer clubs available, and are less certain which shots are best played with them.

So to sharpen up your stewardship of the dummy, try adding these to your bag!

Two basic principles govern an expert's view of a hand:

1. If the contract is comfortable, look for bad breaks and try to protect yourself against them, and
2. If you face an apparently hopeless contract, determine how the cards need to be distributed, however unlikely, and play on that basis.

The hand below falls into the latter category. Let us take declarer's seat and examine our prospects:

Love All. Dealer West.

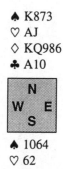

```
            ♠ K873
            ♡ AJ
            ◇ KQ986
            ♣ A10
                N
             W     E
                S
            ♠ 1064
            ♡ 62
            ◇ AJ105
            ♣ K986
```

West	North	East	South
1♡	Dble	2♡	Dble(i)
Pass	3♡(ii)	Pass	4♢
Pass	5♢	All Pass	

(i) A 'responsive' double, showing the values for a positive bid but with no long suit. It usually denies four or more cards in a major

(ii) Trying for 3NT if partner has a stop

After the bidding, during which North might have overstated his hand a touch, West led ♡K and South looked bleakly at dummy. With one heart and two spades (at least) to lose, prospects of making his contract were bleak at best.

Nevertheless, the most talked about hands are often those which superficially have no chance and yet somehow succeed, so South started with gusto.

First he tried three rounds of clubs in case ♣QJ were doubleton. Slightly surprisingly, East showed out on the third round. Declarer returned to hand in trumps and ruffed another club high. Trumps were drawn and South now exited with a spade. This was the position:

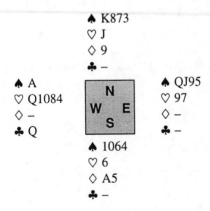

West won ♠A, cashed a heart and continued hearts. Declarer could ruff in dummy and discard his losing spade from hand, thereby restricting his spade losers to one and bringing home the contract.

This was the original layout:

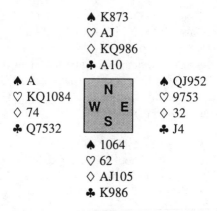

```
                     ♠ K873
                     ♡ AJ
                     ◇ KQ986
                     ♣ A10
     ♠ A                              ♠ QJ952
     ♡ KQ1084          N             ♡ 9753
     ◇ 74          W       E         ◇ 32
     ♣ Q7532           S             ♣ J4
                     ♠ 1064
                     ♡ 62
                     ◇ AJ105
                     ♣ K986
```

West had been thrown in with ♠A and had no good answer. He had to concede a ruff and discard. Undoubtedly, justice was not served, but one can admire South's 'never-say-die' attitude to the play. Note how he had to eliminate all West's diamonds and his own clubs to enable the plan to succeed. Only then could he let West have the lead.

On the other side of the coin, we must be wary of greed.

Greed usually strikes us when we have a nice easy contract, so we are on the look-out for a couple of overtricks. Not that an overtrick or two will make much difference to our bank balance. Rather, it presents an opportunity to show off our technique, somewhat akin to the shots snooker players are seen making after a frame has been won or lost. Sit South on the hand below and we will examine his 'routine' 4♠ contract:

North/South Game. Dealer North.

♠ 10
♡ 10863
◇ A75
♣ AKQ75

♠ AKJ852
♡ KJ
◇ KJ2
♣ 96

West	North	East	South
–	1♣	Pass	2♠
Pass	3♣	Pass	4♠
All Pass			

The bidding would not please the purist. In particular, why did South feel obligated to jump to 4♠ with a minimum force and a broken suit? Both 3♠ and 3NT appear preferable options. Although we might be able to bid the hand better, no one could argue with the final contract.

West led ◇10 which ran round to declarer's jack. Conscious of the need to avoid a heart switch from East (a good principle wrongly applied), South crossed to one of dummy's club honours and ran ♠10. If it held, he was proposing to return to ◇K and lead out ♠AK. Surely there was no danger attached to this line of play and, if everything broke well, he would win all 13 tricks.

Before reading on, would you like to decide on your own plan, or are you happy enough with the declarer's effort? At the table, West won ♠Q and continued diamonds for East to ruff. A heart was returned and declarer, desperate to prevent West getting in again, put up ♡K, but to no avail. West won ♡A and led another diamond for East to ruff. The final ignominy was that East could take ♡Q to defeat the contract by two tricks.

A long way from the three overtricks that South originally planned.

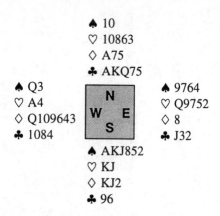

```
              ♠ 10
              ♡ 10863
              ◇ A75
              ♣ AKQ75
  ♠ Q3                         ♠ 9764
  ♡ A4          N              ♡ Q9752
  ◇ Q109643   W   E            ◇ 8
  ♣ 1084        S              ♣ J32
              ♠ AKJ852
              ♡ KJ
              ◇ KJ2
              ♣ 96
```

Notice that even had the spade finesse worked, declarer would have risked his contract by returning to hand with a diamond. Is there a better way? Let us try again from the point where South wins ◇J and follow the excellent premise that, when you have plenty in reserve, it is usually wise to draw trumps. Declarer thus immediately leads out ♠AK. He then turns his attention to clubs.

He plays off dummy's honours discarding ♡J on the third round. Even if spades divide 4-2 and ♣Q is ruffed, declarer will still only lose three tricks. On the actual layout careful play will give South two overtricks, four tricks more than was the case. Sometimes playing cautiously can outperform going for the maximum.

So whenever you appear to have tricks to burn, remember that is the time to beware of bad breaks and play safe. A little extra care can go a long way.

Even if we need a specific layout, it is not always that easy to see how to make use of it. This hand was superbly engineered by Andy Robson:

♠ AQ8
♡ A105
◇ K975
♣ AK6

♠ KJ5
♡ K62
◇ A1084
♣ Q53

Robson had arrived in the fairly awful contract of 6NT and faced an opening lead of ♠ 10. With only 11 tricks apparently available, Robson first looked to diamonds to provide his extra chance. When no honour appeared on the first round of the suit, he seemed to be out for the count. However, he saw a minute chance of success. Can you spot it? Have a good look.

He cashed his spade and club winners and then played two further rounds of diamonds, hoping that West would be forced to take the trick. If West was down to just hearts, and held both the queen and jack of the suit, he would make the slam. Most unlikely I agree, but sometimes it is your day:

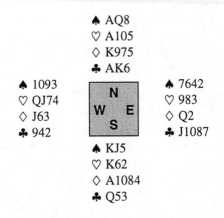

At trick 10, West had to lead a low heart and, as in all good movies, when Robson inserted ♡ 10 there was a happy ending.

If there is a lesson here, it is never to become too despondent, even when a contract seems hopeless. Always be on the lookout for that extra chance, however tiny it might be. And if that seems to be rather obvious advice, it may surprise you to learn that in a world class event only two players found the winning line of play on the above deal.

Here is Robson (South) in action again, partnering me in the Cap Volmac World Pairs of 1994. We were opposed by the Germans, Daniella Von Arnim (West) and Sabine Zenkel (East):

North/South Game. Dealer West.

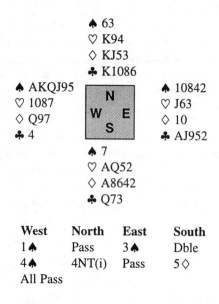

```
              ♠ 63
              ♡ K94
              ◇ KJ53
              ♣ K1086
♠ AKQJ95                    ♠ 10842
♡ 1087          N           ♡ J63
◇ Q97        W   E          ◇ 10
♣ 4             S           ♣ AJ952
              ♠ 7
              ♡ AQ52
              ◇ A8642
              ♣ Q73
```

West	North	East	South
1♠	Pass	3♠	Dble
4♠	4NT(i)	Pass	5◇
All Pass			

(i)   For the minors

We reached a very tight contract of 5◇. This was due to two aggressive actions, the first being Robson's take out double of 3♠, and the second my decision to bid 4NT asking partner to choose his better minor. West led ♣4. Zenkel was aware that this was likely to be a singleton, but she decided not to rise with ♣A just in case her partner had ♣43. After all, she appeared to have two certain club tricks in any case, so what could go wrong? Little did she know.

South won ♣Q and played ◇A and a diamond finessing the jack (West surely had ◇Q for her opening bid). After drawing the last trump, Robson ran the hearts and made the clever play of discarding a *spade* from dummy. This was the situation he had reached:

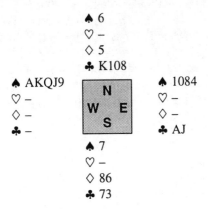

At this point, he led ♠7. If West won the trick, she would have to concede a ruff and discard, whilst East had the equally unpalatable option of a club setting up dummy's king. Either way, eleven tricks would result.

Occasionally spotting your extra chance will result in conceding extra tricks, as Bobby Levin (USA) found out to his cost:

Playing in the Spingold Final (America's most prestigious tournament), you arrive in 3NT and receive ♠K lead. Superficially, the contract depends upon bringing in the diamond suit, but Bobby Levin (who won the Macallan International in 1994), saw an extra chance.

If West held ♡K10x, you would make five tricks in hearts by finessing twice. That would be nine tricks in total, without recourse to diamonds. The only problem is that you seem unable to test this possibility, without risking instant defeat when East has ♡K. Levin found a neat solution.

He won ♠A and led ♡Q at trick two. If West held the king he would surely cover the queen, now declarer could test diamonds, with the heart suit in reserve should it prove necessary. In practice West did not cover ♡Q so Levin correctly assumed that East held ♡K. He rose with the ace and tackled diamonds without success.

This was the full deal:

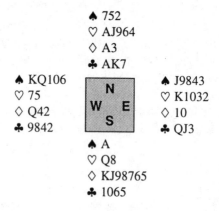

```
                    ♠ 752
                    ♡ AJ964
                    ◇ A3
                    ♣ AK7
   ♠ KQ106                          ♠ J9843
   ♡ 75              N              ♡ K1032
   ◇ Q42          W   E            ◇ 10
   ♣ 9842            S              ♣ QJ3
                    ♠ A
                    ♡ Q8
                    ◇ KJ98765
                    ♣ 1065
```

Because of Levin's heart play, the defence was able to organise a second trick in the suit, thus defeating the contract by three, or 300 points. Levin's bright shot had produced a 3 IMP loss for his team. Not critical normally, but when the scores were compared, his team had lost by 3 IMPs. Who said ignorance is bliss?

School prizes were as rare to me as Oscars once were to Steven Spielberg. On the odd occasion where my academic prowess was considered worthy of reward, I was disappointed to find that all I received was a book token. Being one of life's non-readers, the prize felt more like a punishment. Nevertheless at least the choice of material was easy – Sherlock Holmes.

I suppose the writing of Sir Arthur Conan Doyle must appeal to the bridge mind. The similarities between a Holmes mystery and a tough bridge hand are manifold.

In both we have certain clues, and to be successful we must draw the correct inferences from them. Let me give you a classic of the genre:

Love All. Dealer North.

```
              ♠ K4
              ♡ AJ5
              ◇ Q9742
              ♣ K43

                  N
               W     E
                  S

              ♠ AJ73
              ♡ Q1093
              ◇ A3
              ♣ J107
```

West	North	East	South
–	1◇(i)	Pass	1♡
Pass	2♡	Pass	3NT
All Pass			

(i)   North/South were playing a strong 1NT.

Sitting South, you arrive in the optimum contract of 3NT and West leads a club to East's ace. A club is returned to the jack, queen and dummy's king. You cross to ◇A to run ♡10; it holds as does ♡Q. Everything has gone smoothly to date, but you are still one trick short of your contract if hearts do not break evenly.

Maybe West has ◇K, so you play a diamond to the 10 and queen, but East produces the king. East switches to ♠10 which runs to dummy's king. You try ♡A, but East shows out. No ninth trick there either. A low diamond comes next in the hope of finding a 3-3 division of the suit. No luck, West discards a club.

East now continues with the ♠5 and you have to decide whether to finesse ♠J or rise with the ace. At first glance, the finesse is much more attractive; before we take the plunge, though, let's see how Sherlock Holmes would reason. First, he would attempt to picture the opposing distribution. He would conclude in this case that East held four diamonds, two clubs and two hearts, leaving five cards in spades.

Secondly, he would examine any clues from the bidding. Do I hear you say 'There was no East/West bidding?'.

True, but remember the story about the stolen race-horse Silver Blaze.

'Did you note the curious behaviour of the dog in the night Watson?', queried Holmes

'But the dog did nothing in the night.'

'That was the curious behaviour. If a stranger had stolen the horse, the dog would have barked. Therefore, the horse was stolen by the trainer who was known to the dog'.

Here East did not bid over 1♢, and yet if he held the following:

> ♠ Q10985
> ♡ 76
> ♢ KJ85
> ♣ A8

he would surely have overcalled 1♠.

Therefore, deducing that East could not hold ♠Q, declarer rose with ♠A and dropped the queen in West's hand:

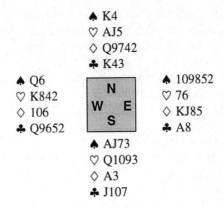

♠ K4
♡ AJ5
◇ Q9742
♣ K43

♠ Q6
♡ K842
◇ 106
♣ Q9652

♠ 109852
♡ 76
◇ KJ85
♣ A8

♠ AJ73
♡ Q1093
◇ A3
♣ J107

Observe all details and note negative inferences with care, not a bad slogan for a bridge player!

Bearing in mind the above deal, how would my hero have tackled the following problem?

Game All. Dealer West.

♠ 876
♡ Q4
◇ AKJ7
♣ 10863

♠ A43
♡ AK10865
◇ 1092
♣ Q

West	North	East	South
Pass	Pass	Pass	1♡
Pass	2◇	Pass	3♡
Pass	4♡	All Pass	

An aggressive auction has carried South to a marginal game on minimal values. Still, there is plenty of hope, as superficially the contract only requires West to hold ◇ Q and for hearts to behave.

West begins the defence with ♣ A and switches most annoyingly to ♠ Q. A second round of clubs would have left an easy task. Declarer wins ♠ A and draws trumps in three rounds, East having ♡ Jxx. What next? Time to bring in Holmes again.

'Where is ◇ Q, that is the question? Under normal circumstances we should take the simple finesse, but there are clues available that tell us to change our strategy. West is likely to hold ♣ AK (because of the lead), and ♠ QJ (when he switched at trick two). Not interesting in itself, until you put it with the fact that he *passed as dealer*. He surely cannot have ◇ Q as well, so the finesse will not work.'

However unlikely it is to succeed, we must play East to have a doubleton ◇ Q and lead out ◇ AK. If the queen falls we can claim:

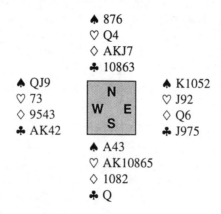

```
              ♠ 876
              ♡ Q4
              ◇ AKJ7
              ♣ 10863
♠ QJ9                        ♠ K1052
♡ 73          ┌─────┐        ♡ J92
◇ 9543        │  N  │        ◇ Q6
♣ AK42        │W   E│        ♣ J975
              │  S  │
              └─────┘
              ♠ A43
              ♡ AK10865
              ◇ 1082
              ♣ Q
```

'However, here is a conundrum. Despite the above deductions, one should still take a finesse in diamonds, Watson. Why?'

Well, can *you* see why you should take a diamond finesse?

The answer lies in the layout of the suit:

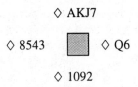

◊ AKJ7

◊ 8543   ◊ Q6

◊ 1092

To maximise the number of tricks, one should drop ◊ 108 under the ace and king. Then cross back to the South hand via a club ruff, and lead up to dummy's ◊ J7 taking the marked finesse against West's ◊ 9. This produces an extra trick.

Should one play 'normally', the suit will be blocked by South's ◊ 10. Attention to detail is an asset for detectives and bridge players alike.

And now for something completely different ….

I rarely take the role of kibitzer, but recently I found myself watching a friend play a practice session, prior to a big event. I say 'role' of kibitzer, because I do not believe that one should be seen and not heard (I never did!), preferring to play a speaking part in the proceedings.

The first half hour passed by without scope to show my 'brilliance' and analytical ability. Then opportunity knocked:

East/West Game. Dealer South.

♠ A72
♡ Q105
◊ AKQJ10
♣ 96

♠ Q98653
♡ 7
◊ 86
♣ K875

West	North	East	South
–	–	–	Pass
1♣	Dble	1♡	3♠
Pass	4♠	All Pass	

No one was entirely confident what strength of hand was indicated by 3♠.
Was it pre-emptive trying to keep the opposition out of the bidding or was
it invitational, and thus a little stronger than 2♠? North took the practical
view and raised to game (just in case).

West led ♡A and continued the suit when his partner encouraged with the
eight. Declarer ruffed and played ♠5, on which West obligingly produced
the king. The ace having being won in dummy, a second round of spades
followed with West predictably showing out.

Now declarer tried to cash dummy's diamonds in the vain hope that East
would have to follow four times. Then South could pitch three losing
clubs. It was not to be, East ruffed the third diamond and switched to a
club. West soon gathered in two tricks and defeat had to be faced:

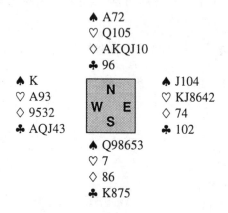

```
                    ♠ A72
                    ♡ Q105
                    ◇ AKQJ10
                    ♣ 96
      ♠ K                          ♠ J104
      ♡ A93           N            ♡ KJ8642
      ◇ 9532      W       E        ◇ 74
      ♣ AQJ43         S            ♣ 102
                    ♠ Q98653
                    ♡ 7
                    ◇ 86
                    ♣ K875
```

'Couldn't make that hand' announced my ex-friend.

I coughed in a way to be noticed without appearing to barge into the
discussion. It had the desired effect.

'Well, I couldn't, could I?' South duly repeated.

Taking what was clearly intended as a rhetorical question as my cue, I entered the fray. Clearing my throat, I began my speech.

'You must keep East off lead because, as soon as he gets in, the automatic club switch will defeat the contract. Somehow he has to be stopped from doing that. The way to achieve it is rather neat. Duck the king of spades when West plays it on the first round of trumps. If he presses on with hearts, you can ruff, draw trumps and cash the diamonds. Any other continuation can be handled just as easily.

I deduced the remainder of the kibitzer's role from the look on South's face. Fortunately the door was close by ....

Finally, always ensure that you decode the defenders' signals. If you fail to pay attention, they will know more than you! Here are a couple of rather sophisticated examples of the theme.

What springs to mind when you think of Belgium? You can't complete the word before my mind has consumed vast quantities of chocolate. However, in a recent survey, Belgians were notable for just one thing – their ability to drink alcohol.

In that respect they are world leaders. What about bridge, I hear you ask? Sadly they are also-rans in that department (maybe the two facts are connected). As far as I know, they have never won a medal of any sort, despite competing in every championship for at least twenty years.

However, do not garner the impression that their card play is at fault. It is the bidding that lets them down. For proof of this, watch their top player, Oliver Nève, handle 3NT on the next deal:

Love All. Dealer South.

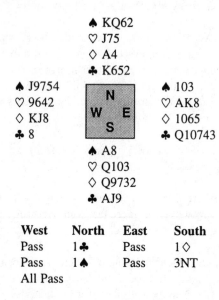

♠ KQ62
♥ J75
♦ A4
♣ K652

♠ J9754   ♠ 103
♥ 9642   ♥ AK8
♦ KJ8   ♦ 1065
♣ 8   ♣ Q10743

♠ A8
♥ Q103
♦ Q9732
♣ AJ9

West	North	East	South
Pass	1♣	Pass	1♦
Pass	1♠	Pass	3NT
All Pass			

Tipped off by the auction, West got away to the best opening lead of a heart. East quickly took ♥AK and returned the suit, putting South on play.

The 'natural' line is to tackle diamonds, hoping that East holds the king, but Nève spotted something in West's carding which caused him to change tack.

On the last heart, West carefully *followed with* ♥9, proclaiming interest in a higher-ranking suit. As this could not be spades, declarer concluded that he was signalling possession of ♦K to his partner.

Thus, South led a club to the king and successfully finessed ♣J, on which West pitched a spade. Then came ♣A, forcing a diamond discard.

Declarer cashed three top spades before giving up a spade to West. He could win his last heart, but had to lead away from ♦KJ in the two-card ending.

South had his antennae working overtime, as did declarer on our final deal:

North/South Game. Dealer North.

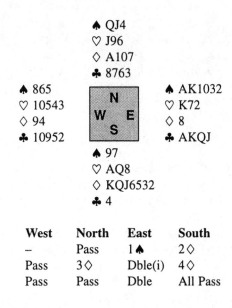

♠ QJ4
♥ J96
♦ A107
♣ 8763

♠ 865
♥ 10543
♦ 94
♣ 10952

♠ AK1032
♥ K72
♦ 8
♣ AKQJ

♠ 97
♥ AQ8
♦ KQJ6532
♣ 4

West	North	East	South
–	Pass	1♠	2◊
Pass	3◊	Dble(i)	4◊
Pass	Pass	Dble	All Pass

(i)   For takeout

East thought he had the opponents where he wanted them, but adept declarer play caused his downfall. With 20 points and two good suits, many players would open 2♠ on the East hand. It will come as no surprise that this bid was not available to East, as 2♠ showed a weak hand. However, nothing terrible happened and, via a takeout double of 3◊, he could accurately describe his shape and values.

When South pressed on to the four level, East had had enough. It was time to teach him a lesson. West led a low spade to the jack and king and a couple of top clubs followed. Apparently declarer must lose a heart and a spade, to go with the two tricks already conceded, but sometimes the eye can be deceived. South crossed to ◊A, finessed ♡Q and followed with an avalanche of diamonds, reducing everyone to three cards.

East was perfectly aware of the problem he was about to face. Declarer had envisaged this ending, with East due to discard:

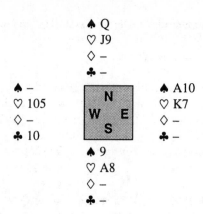

How should East defend? He cannot bare ♡K, otherwise South would lay down ♡A, so he keeps two hearts and ♠A. Then, declarer simply leads a spade, and East has to concede the last two tricks. Check-mate.

But East was a clever cookie. He had worked out what would happen, so he sought to create the impression that he had been dealt:

♠ AK1032
♡ K752
◇ 8
♣ AKQ

Therefore, he discarded a heart early in the proceedings, and hung on to ♣J. This was the actual position with four cards remaining:

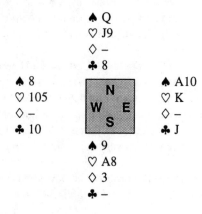

On ◊ 3, West, North and East all discarded spades. If declarer exited with
♠ 9, East would cash ♣ J to defeat the contract. How could South tell what
to do?

It is no use looking to the cards played by East to give any useful clues,
because he is trying to fool you. However, West's carding is a different
matter. To help his partner, particularly in the early play, West will signal
his distribution. Thus, when facing this type of situation, make sure you
watch *all* the small cards. They often provide the guidance you need in the
end-game.

On this occasion, West followed with ♣5 on the first round, before
completing a 'peter' with ♣2 on the second. He was dutifully showing
that he held four clubs. As it turns out, this information is vital to declarer,
for he can then calculate that East still retains a club at the death. Thus he
laid down ♡ A and dropped the king.

East had committed the perfect crime, but sadly his accomplice spilled the
beans. Even so, it required an astute piece of detective work to solve the
case!

There has been a great deal to digest in this chapter, so I have summarised
the major points below for ease of reference. To assist your declarer play
in future, therefore, remember the following:

1. When the contract appears comfortable, protect yourself against bad
    breaks.
2. When the contract looks hopeless, seek the layout you require and go
    for it!
3. Always be aware of extra chances, however small.
4. Be on the look-out for eliminations and end-plays.
5. Do not miss inferences from the opponents' bidding, or lack of it.
6. Make sure you keep the 'danger' hand off lead.
7. Keep a close eye on the cards played by the defence.

If you can absorb all the above, and apply them assiduously at the table,
you will be 'scratch' in a matter of months!

13

WHEN TO FLICK
THE SWITCH

You see them every week in your local Tescos – the queue-hoppers. Not that I am completely blameless here, often dragging my long-suffering wife from one check-out to another, or insisting that I look over the various alternatives before the crucial decision is made.

How frustrating when the shopper in front gets a cheque book out and the transaction proceeds at a snail's pace. I will then look around for another line to speed my progress.

What relevance does this have to bridge, I hear you say?! Well, the queue-hopper has an alter-ego and he is the 'suit-switcher'. He will defend every contract in a frenzied effort to find a good suit to lead and, if he fails in one direction, he will lash out in another. This West was one such player:

♠ J95
♡ 1032
◇ J854
♣ AKJ

He had to lead after the following sequence:

West	North	East	South
–	–	–	1NT(i)
Pass	2NT	Pass	3NT
All Pass			

(i)   12-14 points

Not surprisingly, he began with his only four card suit and selected ◇4 (fourth highest). Dummy was a disappointment, as his choice had clearly failed to strike gold:

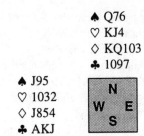

♠ Q76
♡ KJ4
◇ KQ103
♣ 1097

♠ J95
♡ 1032
◇ J854
♣ AKJ

Declarer put on ◇ 10, partner following with ◇ 6. Next came ♣ 10 which ran to West's jack. Time to try another attack, so West switched to ♡ 2, dummy played low and partner's ♡ Q was swallowed by declarer's ace.

Clubs were continued, so our hero had one more string to his bow. A switch to ♠ 5 duly emerged, dummy played low and East's king was taken by the ace. The last club honour was knocked out and West continued his remarkable defence by returning to diamonds, somewhat later than required.

Here is the full deal:

Love All. Dealer South.

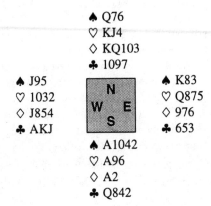

♠ Q76
♡ KJ4
◇ KQ103
♣ 1097

♠ J95
♡ 1032
◇ J854
♣ AKJ

♠ K83
♡ Q875
◇ 976
♣ 653

♠ A1042
♡ A96
◇ A2
♣ Q842

When facing a tricky contract, such as the one South had to contend with here, a defender such as West is declarer's biggest ally. He will flit around from suit to suit finding the missing honours for you; you give him the lead, and he'll do the rest.

Let us go back to the beginning and re-run the defence. No one can see into the cards, so, despite being an unfortunate lead, we will stick with West's actual selection of a diamond. When in with ♣J at trick two, however, we diverge. Rather than go on a treasure-hunt for partner's suit, we play diamonds, letting South have ◇A. After all, the damage we have inflicted on the diamond suit has already been done.

Declarer grinds on with clubs, so we cash our last honour before once more exiting in diamonds, forcing declarer to discard, say, a spade. This is the position we have reached:

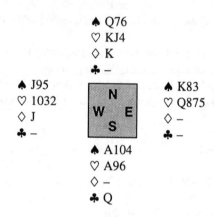

```
              ♠ Q76
              ♡ KJ4
              ◇ K
              ♣ –
  ♠ J95          N          ♠ K83
  ♡ 1032      W     E       ♡ Q875
  ◇ J            S          ◇ –
  ♣ –                       ♣ –
              ♠ A104
              ♡ A96
              ◇ –
              ♣ Q
```

Without second sight, South now plays a spade to the ten and West's jack, who persists with his final diamond. After winning in dummy, South crosses to ♠A (in case ♠K falls), takes ♣Q and finishes by taking the heart finesse. When East produces ♡Q the contract is defeated.

West's second approach, that of the 'Tortoise', has achieved more than his first when he raced from one suit to another (the 'Hare'). It sometimes requires great patience to sit back and let declarer do the work for himself, but it is very often the winning approach. (Maybe I can put that into practice at the supermarket and stick to my original check-out!)

Of course, if defence was that one-dimensional, i.e. lead a suit and stick with it regardless, the play would be totally predictable. Instead there are many opportunities for individual flair. Take the West cards for example, and see what you can think of on this deal:

North/South Game. Dealer West.

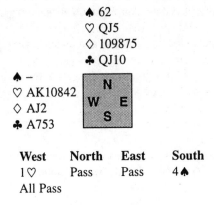

♠ 62
♡ QJ5
◇ 109875
♣ QJ10

♠ –
♡ AK10842
◇ AJ2
♣ A753

West	North	East	South
1♡	Pass	Pass	4♠
All Pass			

The auction has been a big disappointment. When it began, there was hope of a slam if partner had the right hand. Now you are confined to defending South's game contract.

You have been brushed aside in the bidding but this is your chance for revenge. On your lead of ♡A, East follows with ♡3, suggesting an odd number. It is unlikely he holds a singleton, but you never know. Is there any danger in continuing with ♡K, as dummy will be difficult to reach even if you establish ♡Q?

It looks safe enough, doesn't it? Have I tempted you into playing a second heart, or is there a devilish trap? Look at the full hand, and see what happens:

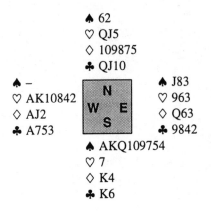

♠ 62
♡ QJ5
◇ 109875
♣ QJ10

♠ –
♡ AK10842
◇ AJ2
♣ A753

♠ J83
♡ 963
◇ Q63
♣ 9842

♠ AKQ109754
♡ 7
◇ K4
♣ K6

Declarer ruffs ♡K and draws trumps. He plays ♣K, which you have to duck in order to prevent dummy's tricks being reached. However, you have only postponed a grizzly fate. Another club appears, which you win ....

There is nothing else for it. Cash ◊A and concede with good grace.

At the table, West found a great switch at trick two, which avoided this end-play. Can you see what it was?

She led ♣3!

Declarer won in hand, drew trumps and backed a club, but West was in control. She won ♣A and led ♡K, forcing South to ruff and lead away from ◊K.

I believe that the ability to spot if and when to change tack is one of the fundamentals of defence. Unfortunately, I have never been able to work out an effective set of principles to govern this decision. Maybe we have no choice but to play it by ear!

14
WELL, WHO WAS
THE GREATEST?

Who is the greatest player of all time? This is hard to assess with any real objectivity in a game where partnerships dominate, but nevertheless many of us love to speculate.

In my opinion, there are three candidates; Benito Garozzo and Pietro Forquet from Italy, two members of the famous 'Blue Team', plus Bob Hamman from the US. Hamman is still playing with a consistency that Paul Gascoigne would be delighted to emulate. He has a fantastic 'bridge brain', seeing situations with amazing clarity. He is still able, after 30 years at the top, to apply huge powers of concentration and thus solve the toughest of problems.

His bidding has never quite graced the heights of his card play. Of my three candidates, Forquet was surely the best bidder. However, Hamman does have one 'golden rule', which is this gem:

'If you have a choice of contracts to play and 3NT is one of them, always choose it.'

It is generally easier to steal tricks in a no trump game than any other. Add to this the fact that 3NT is shielded from bad breaks, and you can see why his advice is sound. South, an obvious 'Hammanite', collected a fine result on the next deal:

Love All. Dealer North.

♠ 7
♡ A5432
◇ KJ94
♣ K42

♠ KQ6
♡ K97
◇ 86
♣ AJ986

West	North	East	South
–	1♡	1♠	2♣
2♠	3♣	Pass	3NT
All Pass			

North opened his 11-point hand, a reasonable decision when a simple re-bid is available (2◇). South bid 2♣ over East's inference, and after a couple of 'courtesy raises', he was at the crossroads.

South had two options: bid 4♡ with his excellent support, or try 3NT and trust to luck. As per the theory of Mr. Hamman, 3NT was duly attempted. South was wishing for a spade lead from West, but no such luck.

The ◇7 settled on the table, giving declarer an anxious wait before North tabled a host of stops in the suit. 'Thank you, what an excellent partner you are', South must have thought. Before it was time to break out the champagne, though, the contract had to be made.

Dummy played low on the lead and East produced ◇5, so South's ◇8 was an unlikely winner. It is good tactics to fire back the suit when an unsuccessful lead is made, so declarer returned a diamond. West won ◇A and switched to a heart to the queen and king. Time for clubs.

A club to the king was followed by one to the jack, West showing out. Declarer ducked a heart but this time East discarded. Another heart was taken in dummy by the ace leaving this position:

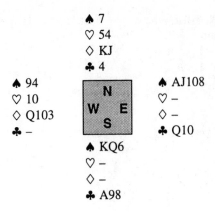

Declarer had lost two tricks to date. He took ◇ K, on which East and South pitched spades. A club to the ace and a second club forced East to cash ♠ A and give South the balance.

Not only did 3NT succeed, but 4♡ would have been defeated by the bad trump break. One for Hamman. This was the full deal:

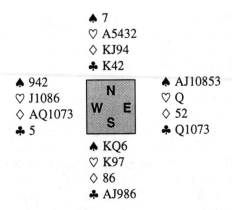

And my 'Greatest'? Benito Garozzo, the complete player – simply the best.

In their period of dominance, the Italian 'Blue Team' had three of the finest players of all time. Now, well into his sixties, Garozzo is still at the top and won the 1992 Cap Volmac World Pairs in partnership with Billy Eisenberg (USA).

Garozzo is credited with one of *the* most spectacular pieces of defence. Can you equal him?

Love All. Dealer South.

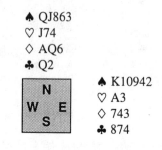

```
              ♠ QJ863
              ♡ J74
              ◊ AQ6
              ♣ Q2
                              ♠ K10942
           N                  ♡ A3
        W     E               ◊ 743
           S                  ♣ 874
```

West	North	East	South
–	–	–	1◊
Pass	1♠	Pass	2◊
Pass	3◊	Pass	3NT
All Pass			

You are East, and your partner leads ♣5 (fourth highest from an honour). Declarer puts up ♣Q and plays ♣6 himself. A spade to the ace is followed by a diamond to the queen and ♠Q. You decide to win ♠K, declarer pitching a heart, how do you proceed?

Let us consider all our options in detail. We could return a club, but as partner led a low club and not the jack, declarer must have at least the ♣KJ. With two spades and one club already established, he would rapidly have nine tricks. What about a heart switch? Well, South felt confident enough about his stop to discard one on the spades, so there does not seem to be a weakness there. A spade return would let declarer win ♠J and lead a club. No good. Having logically dismissed everything else, Garozzo played a diamond, declarer's suit! This is how the cards lay:

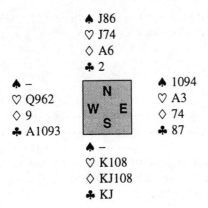

South was in a quandary. He could win the diamond in hand, blocking the suit, but that did not look attractive. Instead, he won ◊A. He could not take ♠J without setting up five tricks for the defence (three spades and two aces), so he tried a heart.

Again, Garozzo was alive. He rose with ♡A and played a heart back! When declarer attempted to establish his ninth trick in clubs, West could cash two hearts and defeat the contract.

This was the full deal:

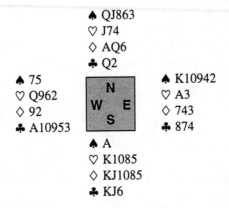

A truly remarkable defence by Garozzo which many consider to be one of the most brilliant ever. Not because it was sensational or clever, but because it required incredible vision and clarity of thought. My case rests.

If doubt exists about the greatest player, there is no question who is the leading showman on the bridge scene. That honour goes to Zia Mahmood – mind you, not even he could have written the script for what happened on the Canberra ....

It has often been said that you make your own luck at bridge and one person who would certainly agree with that is Zia Mahmood.

In a television bridge competition a few years ago, he came to the last hand requiring a slam to overhaul Sami Kehela. He was sitting West and anxiously picked up this hand:

♠ AQ2
♡ J1073
◇ A42
♣ KJ4

Not too bad at all, and definitely giving him a chance of what was required. North dealt and passed, so did East and then South. Zia contemplated his situation.

How likely was it that his partner, who did not hold the values for an opening, would have a sufficiently good hand to make a slam? Not very probable thought he. Gambling on his luck, he passed the hand out! He knew that the cards would have to be re-dealt and he was just trusting to luck that there was a slam in them.

Sure enough, this was the re-dealt hand:

Game All. Dealer North.

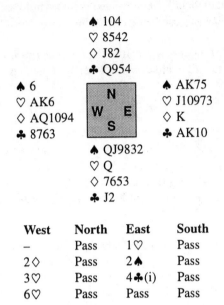

```
                    ♠ 104
                    ♡ 8542
                    ◊ J82
                    ♣ Q954
      ♠ 6                          ♠ AK75
      ♡ AK6           N            ♡ J10973
      ◊ AQ1094     W     E         ◊ K
      ♣ 8763          S            ♣ AK10
                    ♠ QJ9832
                    ♡ Q
                    ◊ 7653
                    ♣ J2
```

West	North	East	South
–	Pass	1♡	Pass
2◊	Pass	2♠	Pass
3♡	Pass	4♣(i)	Pass
6♡	Pass	Pass	Pass

(i)   Cuebid

East was the Swedish star, P. O. Sundelin, North was Sami Kehela (Canada) and I was South, holding my usual collection.

Once Sundelin had opened the bidding, Zia had to bid a slam regardless of whether he thought it would make or not. He was delighted to hear his partner's "reverse" bid of 2♠, showing a good hand. When East later owned up to the ♣A with his cue bid of 4♣, no further discussion was necessary.

In practice, there was little to the play, declarer having 12 easy tricks as soon as ♡Q appeared (two spades, five hearts, three diamonds and two clubs).

So amid great drama, Zia had snatched a most improbable victory on the last hand of all.

Three things struck me. The first was the ability and imagination of Zia to seize his only chance of success. The second was the fact that Kehela held two aces on the 'first' deal and should have opened despite holding only eight points. That would have prevented the possibility of a slam making and guaranteed his success in the competition.

The third point of interest was that in the following series, one year later, I too needed a slam to win the event. What did I pick up?

♠ Q43
♡ 842
◊ Q653
♣ 942

I finished in two diamonds (redoubled by my 'partner', the aforementioned Zia), going two down and losing 1000 points. What was that about making your own luck?

It is amazing what can be achieved when lady luck is your partner for the night!

15

CAN YOU MAKE THE 'OPENING LEAD TEAM'?

To create accurate and telling defences is considered by most players to be the toughest element of bridge. Within defence itself, the toughest of the tough is undoubtedly the selection of a penetrating opening lead. If you find it so, read on ....

The great divide between the United States and Britain is not just confined to the Atlantic Ocean. In sport, as well, we are worlds apart. They do not appreciate cricket, soccer or snooker, whilst we are mystified by baseball. However, American football has acquired something of a cult following over here during the last ten years. One of the more unusual features of the game is the regular changeover of players. Every side has its own 'defense' (pronounced 'deefence' by its true aficionados), 'offense' and 'special' teams who take the field at various points.

If a team gets the ball, on trail the 'offense', until they lose it again and then 'the defense' replace them. Just imagine how a game of cricket would be improved if you were on 'offense'. You bat, score a few runs, and then someone else takes your place to perform all those hours of trailing round at fine leg, whilst you bask in the sun!

Maybe bridge could take up the idea, so our squad will contain the following in future:

Offensive Bidding Team	(you have the cards)
Defensive Bidding Team	(you are making a nuisance of yourself without the cards)
Opening Lead Team	(a small but important task, as we shall see)
Defence Team	(hoping the Opening Leader made a sound choice)
Declarer Team	(the one who gets all the glory!)

Andrew Robson has volunteered himself to be the British 'opening lead' team! Anyone who wishes to dispute Robson's claim to automatic selection, can test themselves on this hand from the BBL Premier League:

East/West Game. Dealer West.

West	North	East	South
1NT(i)	3◇(ii)	4♡	4♠
Pass	Pass	5♡	Pass
Pass	5♠	Pass	Pass
Dble	All Pass		

    (i)   14-16 points
    (ii)   Pre-emptive

You are West, holding:

        ♠ A983
        ♡ AJ107
        ◇ J3
        ♣ KJ9

What would you lead?

After considerable thought, Robson selected ◇J, not an obvious choice by any means. How did it work out?

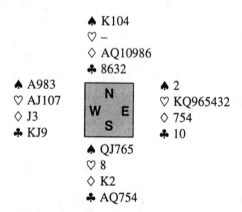

Declarer took the opening lead with ◇K and ruffed a heart in dummy. The ♠K followed, which Robson should have ducked. However, after his amazing lead, one can forgive him anything, and anyway he should have been 'replaced' as soon as ◊ J hit the table! He won ♠A and continued with a second diamond.

South, for reasons best known to himself, tried a further top diamond which West ruffed. A trump lead now removed ♠10 from dummy, and simultaneously killed off the diamond suit.

South had no choice but to play on clubs, and eventually conceded two tricks to West. He was two down. To emphasise just how critical West's lead had been, assume that he started with ♡A.

Declarer ruffs in dummy and leads ♠K. Whether West captures the trick or ducks does not matter. For argument's sake, say he wins ♠A and leads a diamond. After winning ◊ K, South crosses to ♠10 and then returns to hand with ♣A. He draws trumps and claims 12 tricks.

If West ducks ♠K, declarer leads ♠10. The defence can win two trumps, but no more. Robson had worked out that North's diamond suit would be the key, and sought to attack it from the outset. With such foresight, he has my vote for British 'leader'!

To show that even our 'star' man has off days, here are a couple of examples which contributed to ending my interest in the 1995 Spring Foursomes at Stratford.

You (Robson) are West:

1. East/West Game. Dealer East.

> ♠ J973
> ♡ 62
> ◊ AK93
> ♣ AJ7

West	North	East	South
–	–	Pass	1♡
Pass	2◊	Pass	2♡
Pass	3♡	Pass	4♡
All Pass			

What do you lead?

2. North/South Game. Dealer South.

               ♠ J9843
               ♡ 87
               ♢ AQ
               ♣ J973

West	North	East	South
–	–	–	1♡
Pass	4♡	Pass	6♡
All Pass			

Can you find the killing lead?

Answers

1. You have been blessed with almost all the defensive assets, and yet it is still nearly impossible to know what the winning selection may be. It is quite feasible to have a layout where a spade, establishing a 'slow' trick for the defence, a diamond, giving partner a ruff, or a trump, playing passively, may succeed. The only suit which we can rule out for all practical purposes is a club. Here is the actual layout:

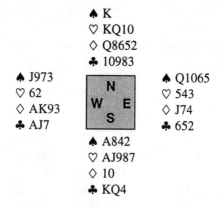

        ♠ K
        ♡ KQ10
        ♢ Q8652
        ♣ 10983

♠ J973   ♠ Q1065
♡ 62   ♡ 543
♢ AK93   ♢ J74
♣ AJ7   ♣ 652

        ♠ A842
        ♡ AJ987
        ♢ 10
        ♣ KQ4

The only effective defence is to begin with a trump at trick one, and continue trumps as soon as you gain the lead. This will prevent declarer from scoring more than one spade ruff and limit his winners to nine. If you start with ◇ A, a trump switch will be too late. Declarer wins ♡K, cashes ♠K and ruffs a diamond. Now after taking ♠A, successive spade and diamond ruffs follow, before a club is led to establish the tenth trick.

2.   Did you lead out ◇ A and trust to luck?

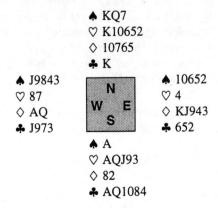

```
                        ♠ KQ7
                        ♡ K10652
                        ◇ 10765
                        ♣ K
          ♠ J9843                      ♠ 10652
          ♡ 87            N            ♡ 4
          ◇ AQ         W     E         ◇ KJ943
          ♣ J973          S            ♣ 652
                        ♠ A
                        ♡ AQJ93
                        ◇ 82
                        ♣ AQ1084
```

Barry Crane, a famous American player (who incidentally directed several TV programmes), once said 'If the opponents bid a slam and I hold an ace, there is no lead problem!' He would have done admirably here.

Is there any scientific way one can arrive at a diamond lead on this hand? I do not believe so, and I am delighted that is so. South took a chance when he simply blasted to a slam, his idea being to conceal his hand from the opposition. It was quite possible that 6♡ was the best contract but, if it was not, he wanted to give himself the extra chance of a blind lead.

Note how a technically 'superior' sequence would pinpoint the diamond losers:

West	North	East	South
–	–	–	1♡
Pass	4♣(i)	Pass	4♠(ii)
Pass	5♡	All Pass	

(i)   A splinter bid, showing a singleton club and a raise to 4♡

(ii) A cuebid showing ♠A, but denying control in diamonds

North/South safely avoid the 'doomed' slam, but lose points on the board to the 'bow-and-arrow' approach at the other table. Personally, I am delighted that, for all the science one can bring to bear on our game, good old-fashioned tactics can still win through. Long may it remain so.

Let me digress for a moment, though. Imagine you are in a nefarious frame of mind, and have decided that you are finished playing by the rules. It is time for a little skulduggery. You summon your partner to discuss methods by which to 'improve your chances'. Having gone along with this hypothesis so far, what would you consider the most important message that could be illegally transmitted?

Nearly all 'systems' designed to cheat have focused on one aspect of the game … the opening lead. Surprised?

To see the power of such an arrangement, consider this hand which I held in the 1996 Rhodes Olympiad. You are West:

♠ AJ106
♡ KJ84
◊ Q73
♣ 82

West	North	East	South
–	–	–	1♡
Pass	2♣	Pass	2NT(i)
Pass	3NT	All Pass	

(i)   Showing 12 to 14 points, balanced hand

The Finnish North/South bid briskly to 3NT and you have to lead. Any of the suits might prove to be the winner or be a total disaster, what you need is a little help from East! Without such an aid, I toyed with spades, hearts and diamonds but was unable to select any of them. In the end, I limply put ♣8 on the table.

This was the full deal:

Love All. Dealer South.

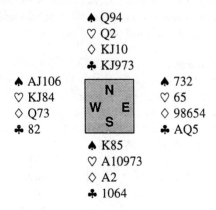

♠ Q94
♥ Q2
♦ KJ10
♣ KJ973

♠ AJ106   ♠ 732
♥ KJ84   ♥ 65
♦ Q73   ♦ 98654
♣ 82   ♣ AQ5

♠ K85
♥ A10973
♦ A2
♣ 1064

In fact, a club is the only lead to give the defence a chance. Declarer was allowed to win the first trick with ♣10, and returned the suit to East's ♣Q.

Quick as a flash (yes, really), Andrew Robson put ♠3 on the table, which naturally enough travelled to the ten and dummy's ♠Q. A further club put East on play again, and a second spade enabled West to scoop three tricks in the suit and defeat the contract.

Of course, it would have been easy if we had a signalling system to ask for a club lead, but hugely less rewarding. It is hard for me to see the appeal of taking many of the unknowns out of the game. Why bother to play at all?

The subject of trump leads is one which deserves a section to itself ....

The greatest advance in tournament play over the last decade is the custom of making one's opening lead face downwards. It is rule designed to eliminate the problems faced by a 'lead out of turn', which is always a nuisance to both defender and declarer alike.

However, there is a little-thought-of side effect which recently occurred to me. The process delays the often less than magic moment when we *see* partner's dreaded lead. It is frequently an anxious time for us, waiting to find out if partner has hit upon the suit we were rooting for, or more probably rooting against (usually trumps!).

I often find, when looking at a couple of potential trump tricks, that partner exposes my assets to declarer. A painful experience to be sure! It is time to give a tip on how to save yourself from impending disaster. You are sitting East:

Love All. Dealer South.

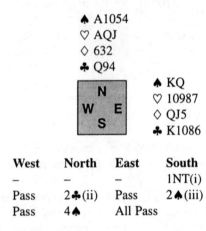

```
            ♠ A1054
            ♡ AQJ
            ◇ 632
            ♣ Q94
                        ♠ KQ
         N              ♡ 10987
      W     E           ◇ QJ5
         S              ♣ K1086
```

West	North	East	South
–	–	–	1NT(i)
Pass	2♣(ii)	Pass	2♠(iii)
Pass	4♠	All Pass	

(i)   12-14 points
(ii)   Stayman for majors
(iii) Four spades, denies four hearts (with both majors, you
       always bid 2♡)

After a fairly routine sequence, West with little to guide him, selects ♠3 as his opening lead. Without this accursed trump on the table, you would have been confident of winning two tricks in the suit, but now there is a serious danger of declarer 'dropping' our second honour. Which spade should we play at trick one?

It is tempting to put up the king in a vain hope to disguise the fact that we possess the queen, but a little thought should lead us away from that conclusion. We clearly need to leave declarer with the impression that West *might* have a spade honour. Whilst it is feasible that he led a trump from ♠Kxx, it is inconceivable that he would select one from ♠Qxx.

Hence, to play ♠K will advertise the fact that we possess ♠Q. It is good defensive technique to play a card which declarer knows we hold. So we win

♠ Q and switch to ◇ Q. At least declarer has a guess, although he is still more likely to guess correctly. Some of the damage done by the lead is irreversible.

Love All. Dealer South.

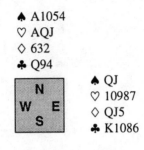

♠ A1054
♡ AQJ
◇ 632
♣ Q94

♠ QJ
♡ 10987
◇ QJ5
♣ K1086

West	North	East	South
–	–	–	1NT
Pass	2♣	Pass	2♠
Pass	4♠	All Pass	

Same sequence, same meanings and the same lead, ♠3! Again, declarer plays a low spade from dummy, what should we do? The 'normal' card from our holding is ♠J, but we must consider the implications as before. If we play any other card than ♠Q, declarer will know we are left with her ladyship and take appropriate action. On this occasion, we play ♠Q to leave declarer to deduce the location of ♠J.

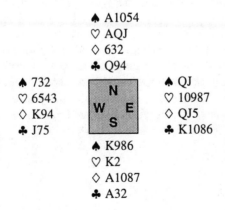

♠ A1054
♡ AQJ
◇ 632
♣ Q94

♠ 732
♡ 6543
◇ K94
♣ J75

♠ QJ
♡ 10987
◇ QJ5
♣ K1086

♠ K986
♡ K2
◇ A1087
♣ A32

Should South misguess the spade layout, sensible defence will set the contract.

Here is another to mull over:

Game All. Dealer South.

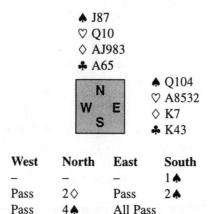

♠ J87
♡ Q10
♢ AJ983
♣ A65

♠ Q104
♡ A8532
♢ K7
♣ K43

West	North	East	South
–	–	–	1♠
Pass	2♢	Pass	2♠
Pass	4♠	All Pass	

West leads ♠3, dummy plays low, and you ...?

Looking adoringly at your trump holding, you are disappointed to see the inevitable ... a trump lead from partner. One thing must be avoided, one must not look daggers at partner and throw your card on the table. Having said that, which card should we play? The obvious answer is ♠10, forcing out either declarer's ace or king, but we can all predict what will happen.

Declarer enthusiastically crosses to dummy with a minor suit ace and leads ♠J, letting it ride if we play low. Our trump trick has disappeared, just as we feared when we saw partner's ♠3. To achieve something meaningful, we must ask ourselves, which card does declarer know that we possess? That must be ♠Q (West would surely never lead away from the queen of trumps). We must play that card immediately, despite the fact that it might appear, at first glance, to be ridiculous.

To see how we might gain, let us view the deal from declarer's perspective:

♠ J87
♡ Q10
◇ AJ983
♣ A65

♠ AK962
♡ KJ9
◇ 52
♣ QJ9

West leads ♠3 against your 4♠ contract, you play low in dummy and East produces ♠Q. How would you proceed?

Without knowing there was a devious East lurking in the undergrowth, i.e. yourself, isn't it logical to continue with a low spade at trick two and finesse dummy's ♠8? This would guard against the following layout:

♠ J87

♠ 10543   ♠ Q

♠ AK962

East's bright manoeuvre of putting up ♠ Q at trick one saves the day for the defence. Let us hope it does not inspire too many other leads along the same lines! Here's the full deal:

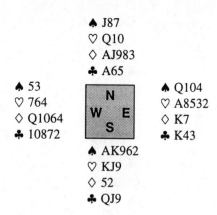

My final comments on trump leads relate to the card we should select. Unlike 'normal' suits, where we would often choose the top of a sequence or from small cards, we have to modify our approach. Why is this?

First, we are not trying to tell partner anything meaningful about our trumps. He knows what the objective of a trump lead is as well as we do. Secondly, we might lose a natural trick, because the risk of partner having an embarrassing holding is magnified.

Always choose your lowest card (unless leading from a doubleton ace or AKx[x]), even if it superficially looks silly. Here is an example which should clear up any confusion:

♠ J108
♡ Q106
◇ Q104
♣ AJ43

You are West and have to select your lead after the following sequence:

West	North	East	South
–	–	–	1♠
Pass	3♠	All Pass	

With bits and pieces everywhere, and the opponents in a partscore, this looks the time for a trump lead, but not ♠J (or ♠10) as normal, because this might occur:

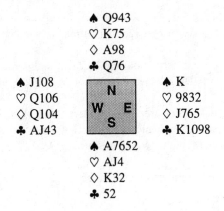

You were right to pick a safe lead, but ♠J or ♠10 will enable declarer to pick up trumps for no loss if he plays low in dummy. However, the lead of ♠8 guarantees the defence at least one spade trick.

Occasionally, you will engineer a coup, as West did on the hand below:

North/South Game, and 60. Dealer South.

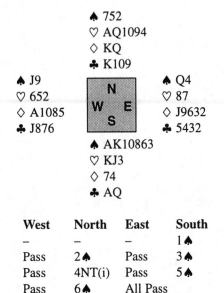

West	North	East	South
–	–	–	1♠
Pass	2♠	Pass	3♠
Pass	4NT(i)	Pass	5♠
Pass	6♠	All Pass	

(i)   Blackwood

North\South rather greedily rejected their safe rubber, in search of a slam bonus. As the cards lay it appeared that nothing could stop them, until ....

West thought long and hard about the bidding, and decided that his best chance was a trump. He selected ♠9, of course, with startling results.

East put up ♠Q, and declarer took the ace. Had West led a singleton spade, mused South, it certainly appeared that way. Prepared to back his judgement, South crossed to ♠A, and finessed ♠10.

West has dined out on this story ever since!